BRIDGING
THE
SUTRAS AND TANTRAS

A collection of ten minor works by

Gyalwa Gendun Drub
the First Dalai Lama (1391-1474)

Compiled and translated

by Glenn H. Mullin

et alia

Illustrated by the late Kevin Rigby

**Gabriel/Snow Lion,
Ithaca, New York U.S.A.**

Snow Lion Publications
are published by
Gabriel Press
under the imprint
Gabriel/Snow Lion
122 S. Cayuga St.
Ithaca, New York, 14850 U.S.A.

First Published by
Tushita Books 1981, India

Library of Congress
Catalog Card # 81-86166

ISBN-0-937938-11-4 Paper
ISBN-0-937938-12-2 Cloth

Snow Lion Publications
are dedicated to
His Holiness Tenzin Gyatso
the Fourteenth Dalai Lama of Tibet

Contents

Preface

by Lama Tubten Yeshe

The collected works of the First Dalai Lama are a veritable mine of precious instruction for the practice of the Buddhadharma. Although written more than four centuries ago, their message vibrates with a meaning as relevant today as at the time of their composition.

The first work in this present volume of translations is *Crushing the Forces of Evil to Dust*, a poem on the life of Buddha Shakyamuni, a source of great inspiration. Sometimes our study and practice of Dharma may lack direction and be clouded by doubt and confusion. If at such moments we look to the life of Buddha to see how he renounced cyclic existence, dedicated himself to the elevation of the world and applied himself to the six transcending perfections, our own spiritual quest is made clear. Correct practice becomes simple and every action of body, speech and mind automatically integrates with the intent of the fully Enlightened Ones.

Notes on Spiritual Transformation, an explanation of the *lo-jong* (Tib. bLo-spyong) method as embodied in the short precept *Spiritual Transformation in Seven Points* (Tib. *bLo-spyong-don-bdun-ma*), provides advice particularly useful for our day-to-day life. It is not exotic nor poetic,

but purely pragmatic: its subject is how to transform one's
every activity into a spiritually significant event, into a
method of opening the heart toward others. This is right
livelihood, right action, in the deeper sense of the word.
Especially, in the present age of social and economic unrest
when so few conditions support spiritual practice and so
many oppose it, when the use of material resources, which
are meant to support life, is exaggerated to obsession, the
lo-jong teaching is most useful. To live we must use material
things, but at present the world has largely degenerated into
seeing materialistic grasping as the supreme answer to existence. This is the environment in which we ourselves must
live and practice. *Lo-jong* is a method very effective in
transforming aggressive and grasping circumstances into
aids on the path. Unless we have a method that can be
applied in every situation, it will be very difficult to tame
the wild elephant of the mind in this twentieth century.

Another important aspect of the *lo-jong* teaching is that it
is practised by all four sects of Tibetan Buddhism. The
lineage was originally brought to Tibet by Atisha in the
mid-eleventh century and formed the basis of the ancient
Kadam Tradition (Tib. bKa'-g̈dams-kyi-lugs), but from the
Kadampa teachers it gradually found its way into all four
Tibetan sects. Many commentaries to it can be found in the
corpus of literature of all Tibetan traditions. This wide-
range applicability of the *lo-jong* teaching in Tibet is doubly
relevant, for it means that not only is the First Dalai Lama's
Notes on Spiritual Transformation acceptable to all students
and practitioners of Tibetan Buddhism regardless of sect,
a certain universality of the *lo-jong* doctrine is suggested.
As well as being of value to all traditions of Buddhism,
it can be used and applied by all peoples interested in true
spiritual development. Whether or not one is a Buddhist,
whether or not one believes in the traditional interpretations

of Buddha, Dharma and Sangha, whether or not one is formally religious, the *lo-jong* teachings can be beneficially implemented.

The material in Chapter III deals with the Buddhist view of emptiness as propagated by the Indian sage Nagarjuna. The search for the wisdom of emptiness, the insight which reveals the ultimate nature of mind and all phenomena, which are empty of all the characteristics we ascribe to them, is the heart of the Buddhist path; for it is this wisdom that gives ultimate liberation from karma, delusion and compulsive cyclic experiences.

Song of the Eastern Snow Mountains is one of the First Dalai Lama's most popular writings. This poem reveals the purity of the author's devotion and shows, firstly, the correct attitudes to be held toward one's own spiritual teachers and, secondly, wrong attitudes often held toward other spiritual traditions. Many people who embrace a particular religious tradition become fanatical in their practice and in their relationship toward others. They think that they are the cream of the world and that people of any other spiritual tradition are like pigs. Dharma practice is designed to cultivate liberal, open attitudes, to encourage harmony amongst people; but sometimes it has the opposite effect. We should look upon all other living beings with love and respect, regardless or whether they are religious or not, Buddhist or not, our sect or not. It is very important to have respect and devotion for our own teacher, our own Lama or Guru; but this should be done in a reasonable way. By seeing his knowledge, compassion and wisdom, and experiencing the beneficial effects he brings into our life, we naturally will develop a love and admiration for him. But our own attitude toward him must be kept within a valid perspective. Many people become obsessive toward their teacher, thinking, "He is the greatest of all teachers, all others are inferior to him." In *Song of the Eastern Snow Mountains* the First Dalai Lama is strongly warning us to guard against such sectarian tendencies.

The text on the *Kalachakra Tantra* provides a guide to the nature of the yogas of Highest Tantra. These yogas are both difficult and dangerous for those who are unprepared, yet for the spiritually mature they present a path to the full enlightenment of Buddhahood that can be accomplished in the space of a few years. As stated in the text, one must first train one's mind in the lower practices and then obtain initiation from a fully accomplished master. Only then will the higher methods be effective.

The concluding prayers and advice represent the type of minor writings with which the collected works of most great Lamas are adorned. These short works condense many themes of the spiritual path, and contemplating them naturally causes our mind to focus upon practice.

Many Tibetan scriptures are perhaps designed for and limited to a Tibetan audience. However, this collection transcends cultural and racial barriers. In substance these works are essentially as practical and valid to the Western mind as to the Asian. I have no doubt that they can benefit any true spiritual seeker who reads them with a sincere heart and an open mind.

Lama Tubten Yeshe,
Tushita Meditation Centre,
Dharamsala, H.P. India.
April 27, 1980.

Translator's Introduction

The First Dalai Lama is perhaps one of the most classic examples of the mobility of the Tibetan spiritual hierarchy, especially within the Kadam and New Kadam sects. Born in a cowshed in 1391 as the son of nomadic tribespeople and raised as a shepherd until the age of seven, he was then placed in Nartang Monastery and, although from the humblest of backgrounds, by the middle of his life had become one of the most respected scholar-saints in the country. The titles *Panchen* or 'Supreme Teacher' and *Tamche Kyenpa*, or 'Omniscient One', were prefixed to his ordination name. By the end of his life his prestige was overshadowed by that of no other lama in the land.

On the night of the child's birth the cowshed in which the nomads were taking shelter was attacked by bandits and they were forced to flee for their lives. The mother wrapped her newly born baby in a blanket, hid him between two boulders and disappeared into the night. When the tribe returned the following morning the boy was seen lying unharmed, a huge black raven standing over him and protecting him from a flock of crows and vultures that had gathered. The traditional biographies state that this raven was an emanation of Four-Headed Mahakala, a wrathful form of the Bodhisattva of Compassion that was to act as the First Dalai Lama's main protective deity throughout his life (see Chapter VI, text three).

During his early years the child was constantly seen carving prayers and *mantras* on rocks and boulders as he passed his days earning his living by tending herds of sheep and goats. When asked why he dedicated so much time to carving mystic inscriptions, he replied, "For the benefit of my parents." On being reminded that his parents were still alive, the boy, then five years old, said, "I am inscribing these prayers to the end that the karmic stains of all living beings, all of whom have been my parents, may be purified." Several of these stone-cuttings are said to be still preserved in Tibet.

When the boy was only seven years old his father passed away and his mother, unable to support him, entered him into Nartang Monastery for classical education. He was given pre-novice ordination together with the name Padma Dorje, 'Thunderbolt Lotus', and was placed under several tutors for training. This began with a study of the four main Tibetan scripts, as well as Mongolian, Chinese and Sanskrit.

At the age of fifteen he became a novice monk and was given the name by which he was later to sign his many written works: Gendun Drub. His studies in Nartang were progressing exceptionally well and now included the vast *Par-chin* or "Perfection of Wisdom" teachings, *Uma* or "the doctrine of the middle view of emptiness," as well as *Nam-trel* or "valid knowledge" and an assortment of other Sutrayana and Vajrayana subjects. When Gendun Drub was given the transmission of the *Mandala of the Medicine Buddhas* his teacher received a vision that the young student would gain great attainment. Throughout this training period Gendun Drub performed several meditation sittings daily in addition to annual and periodic retreats.

Upon reaching his twentieth year, Gendun Drub took the *bikkshu* ordination of a full monk. Five years later he completed his studies at Nartang and left for Central Tibet, where he visited Tradruk and Tangboche monasteries. In 1 15 he met with

Lama Tsong Khapa, an exceptional teacher from eastern Tibet who had studied under forty-five masters representing all sects of Tibetan Buddhism and who was teaching a synthesis of these based upon Atisha's (eleventh century) meditative Kadam Order. Gendun Drub had originally been trained as a Kadampa monk and Tsong Khapa's traditional Kadampa approach of combining intellectual and meditative trainings as well as providing a path unifying the exoteric Sutrayana methods with the esoteric Vajrayana techniques, discovered fertile soil in the spirit of the young disciple. On their first meeting Tsong Khapa tore a piece of cloth from his robe and gave it to Gendun Drub with the prophesy that he would be instrumental in preserving the Buddhist *vinaya* in Tibet. Indeed, the collected works of the First Dalai Lama contain two works on *vinaya* that are amongst the most important on the subject to be written by any Tibetan lama before or since and that even today are widely read and studied. Of note, both of these have been printed (in Tibetan) several times in India over the last two decades by the refugee community, each time selling out inconveniently quickly.

The importance of Atisha and Tsong Khapa in Gendun Drub's life—the former as a lineage master and the latter as an immediate teacher—cannot be underestimated. Although he studied with lamas from many different sects, the teachings of these two masters were to be particularly relevant to his personal spiritual life. The second text in this present collection of minor writings of the First Dalai Lama, *Notes on Spiritual Transformation*, is a direct commentary to Atisha's "Spiritual Transformation in the Mahayana Tradition"; and the text of Chapt. IV, *Song of the Eastern Snow Mountains*, is a hymn to Tsong Khapa. Both of these articles demonstrate the respect that Gendun Drub held toward these two adepts.

In total Gendun Drub studied and meditated for twelve years in Central Tibet, receiving many Sutrayana transmissions as well as Vajrayana lineages such as Milarepa's *Six Yogas of*

Naropa, the *Guhyasamaja Tantra*, the *Tantra of Heruka Chakrasambhava*, and so forth. He then returned to Nartang, where he taught and wrote extensively.

Gendun Drub also studied extensively in Padma Choling Monastery. During one transmission his teacher asked him many questions, and Gendun Drub's answers so impressed those present that from this time on he became known as *Tamche Kyenpa* Gendun Drub, or "The All-Knowing Gendun Drub." He received the transmission of the *Kalachakra Tantra* (on which the material in Chapter V is based) while studying in Evam Monastery.

In accordance with prophesy Gendun Drub determined to build Tashi Lhungpo Monastery. In 1447 he entered meditation and prayer and then set about the task of collecting money, materials and craftmen to do the job. Mystic dakinis guided his work of construction, and even the name Tashi Lhungpo came to him in a dream of a dakini. Himself a skilled painter and artist, the images that he had constructed in Tashi Lhungpo's assembly hall stand as evidence of his aesthetic taste. The main image in the temple was that of Maitreya Buddha and stood twenty-five spans in height. Gendun Drub sealed the completion of this with the composition of the prayer herein translated in Chapter VI, text two. On the consecration day, Tashi Lhungpo was clothed in rainbows and a gentle rain of flowers fell from the sky. The year was 1453.

Throughout his life Gendun Drub lived as a simple Kadampa monk dedicating his time to study and meditation. In total he spent almost twenty years in meditational retreats. After gaining realization he guided many disciples along the paths and stages to enlightenment and wrote many scriptures, some of which are merely a few verses and others many hundreds of pages in length.

The First Dalai Lama's death was as moving as was his life. When he reached his eighty-fourth year he summoned his monks to him, gave them final advice and told them he was about to die. Some pleaded with him to use his powers to extend his life-span again, others asked what prayers they should do. "Always bear the teachings of Buddha in mind and for the sake of all living beings apply them to the cultivation of your own stream of being. Remember the doctrines of Tashi Lhungpo. Make every effort to live, meditate and teach in accordance with the true thought of Buddha. This alone can fulfil my wishes." He then entered into tantric meditation. His body began to transform from that of an old man into that of a youth and shone with such brilliance that few could bear even to look at it. Countless miracles occured in the vicinity that night and the following days. He remained sitting in meditation for thirty days there-after, his heart no longer beating nor his breath passing, his body emanating rainbows and great waves of light. Thus his attainment of Buddhahood was made evident.

The following collection of minor texts by the First Dalai Lama contains ten writing from his *Collected Works*. Rather than clutter the anthology with a wad of footnotes I have chosen the materials carefully and structured them according to the Kadampa Order of doctrine classification. The only really diffi-cult text is that in Chapter V (*Notes on Kalachakra*), and to footnote this would require a book in itself. For a philosophical commentary to the nature of Highest Tantra yoga, readers are referred to *The Life and Teachings of Naropa* by H.V. Guenther (Oxford, 1963). Guenther gives tables of the vajra elements in Sanskrit, Tibetan and English, whereas I give them in English only when the terms translate meaningfully and otherwise leave them as mentioned by the First Dalai Lama. My purpose here is to give a sampling of Gelukpa tantric writings; to impose Western academic norms upon the treatise or to use wierd English equivalents for the energies and so forth seems point-less. Gendun Drub's text largely follows Naropa's *Treatise on the Initiations* (*see* Bibliography, page 156), so Guenther's work on Naropa's "Six Yogas" is a valuable supplement to this chapter.

I was at first hesitant to use this Kalachakra material due to its highly esoteric nature. However, most early translators of Tibetan scriptures seem to have been misguided by their infor-mants and as a consequence there is a popular misbelief in the West that the Gelukpa neither care for nor practise the tantras. On the contrary, in fact all sects of Tibetan Buddhism combine trainings in both the Sutrayana and Vajrayana paths, and to present a selection of works by any Tibetan lama, particularly the Dalai Lamas, and not to include both sutra and tantra materials, would be unfair to the author and reader alike, not to mention the translator. With this thought in mind I sent His Holiness a note requesting his permission to include the work in my collection, adding that I thought the text to be sufficiently short to maintain the tantric code of secrecy yet sufficiently detailed to give the intelligent reader a taste of the richness of Highest Tantra language and symbolism. Permission granted, I set about work on the text with Thepo Rinpoche. As several passages in the text were unintelligible to us, we tra-velled to Ganden Shartse Monastery and requested Thepo's tutor Ven. Lati Rinpoche, who at the time of writing is Shartse's abbot (and formerly was a visiting Professor at Virginia University), to give us a brief commentary for translation purposes. We then revised our earlier translation and added a few notes in the opening sections from Ven. Lati Rinpoche's commentary.

Readers unfamiliar with Highest Tantra writings should keep in mind that the sexuality referred to throughout this chapter is merely an organic interpretation of the dual appearance of Being, and of how this duality is seen as one when the mind of love, wisdom and spiritual maturity has been generated. Woman is the goddess Wisdom, and man the Divine Activity of enlightened methods that sport in an eternal dance of fascination with Wisdom, a union that spreads great bliss from the moment of its conception. Sexuality is our deepest instinct, and by using sexual imagery in our meditations we call up some of the most powerful forces at our disposal. Moreover, to be unable to face our own sexuality is to lock ourselves from enlightenment; for the Buddhist enlightenment fundamentally means knowing and understanding all aspects of our body, mind and the seemingly external world.

Readers will please note that any texts quoted by the author are given only in English throughout the translations, with the exception of root tantras that have the same name as the deity of the mandala (eg. , the *Guhyasamaja Tantra*). Each translation is appended with a bibliography of any texts quoted, together with its Tibetan title as given by the First Dalai Lama. The marks (K.) and (T.) respectively indicate whether the work quoted is from the *Kanjur* (*translations of Buddha's Word*) or *Tanjur* (*translations of works by later Indian Buddhist masters*). Any text not marked by either of these is an indigenous Tibetan work. However, in accordance with tradition the First Dalai Lama mainly quotes early Indian scriptures in order to show the lineage of the teaching.

Throughout the introduction I have referred to Gendun Drub as the First Dalai Lama; yet the name was given to him only posthumously, when the Third Dalai Lama turned the Timut Mongols toward Buddhism in 1578. This lama's name was Tamche Kyenpa Sonam Gyatso Palzangpo, or "The All-Knowing and Sublimely Glorious Ocean of Spiritual Energy." Finding this somewhat unwieldly, the Mongolian Khan preferred simply to call him *Ocean* Lama, or, in Mongolian, *Dalai* Lama. The name was then ascribed to his two previous incarnations, making Gendun Drub the first, Gendun Gyatso the second, and Sonam Gyatso the third. The present Dalai Lama, an embodiment of every realization of the path to enlightenment, is fourteenth in this rosary of jewel incarnations.

Glenn H. Mullin
Ganling Cottage,
Dharamsala, India, 1981,
Fifth month of the Iron Bird Year

Chapter I:

Crushing The Forces Of Evil To Dust

A biographical poem on the life of Buddha Shakyamuni

To the myriads of Gurus, Buddhas
and Bodhisattvas I bow down.

A million sunbeams dance from behind the golden mountains;
They pervade and illuminate the world.
Yet more brilliant is the golden body of Buddha
Radiant with the marks and signs of perfection.
May his lotus feet rest always upon the crown of my head.

A weapon cuts through the net of doubt,
Revives the three worlds and terrifies the powers of ignorance.
Such is the voice of Buddha made perfect in sixty ways,
That awakens living beings from the sleep of delusion.

Beyond confusion, purely perceiving thought
And its objects, his mind in a single moment
Sees clearly all things that may be known,
And with love and wisdom gives unfailing protection.

The Noble Shakyamuni gave birth to the precious bodhimind,
Then for three aeons trained under myriads of Buddhas.
Gradually he transcended the paths and stages
And gained enlightenment in this age of conflict.
O Buddha, Lord of Men, I sing your praise.

Later he took birth in the Tushita Pure Land,
Manifest as Shvetaketu, a Supreme Lord.
I bow to he who joyously satiated
Even the gods with the nectar of Dharma.

At that time inspired by a verse
And knowing where, when and how he should manifest,
He proclaimed: "I shall descend to the earth,"
And reminded the gods to rely on awareness.

In order not to leave them without a protector
He then passed his crown to Lord Maitreya.
"You after me will manifest mahabodhi on earth,"
He prophesied, and empowered Maitreya as his regent.

A billion world systems filled with light
As he left Tushita; taking the form of a white elephant,
He entered the womb of She Greater than a Goddess,
Queen Mahamaya, who was engaged in spiritual practice.

A lotus grows in mud but is not stained by mud:
He dwelt in a womb but remained free from its faults.
For there, adorned with the marks and signs of perfection,
He lay as though in a heavenly mansion.

Each of the gods came to him there
And offered his mother a celestial palace.
The gods immediately were blessed with a vision
Of he and his mother present as their guests.

And as his tiny body formed in the womb,
The worldly protectors, such as Brahma and Indra,
Came to him each day, made clouds of offerings
And received from him the transmission of Dharma.

After some days, every flower on earth blossomed,
Men found everywhere precious gems and treasures
And rare medicinal trees appeared:
The thirty-two wondrous omens were manifest.

The time had come for his birth in Lumbini
And Queen Mahamaya walked in her garden.
Brahma and Indra followed to attend him
And immortal goddesses filled the skies with offerings.

In the Lumbini Gardens stood a *plaksha* tree,
And as Mahamaya rested her hand on a branch
The child slipped painlessly out from her side
Like a flash of lightning from a white cloud.

Brahma and Indra took him up in their arms,
Washed him in scented waters and offered him flowers.
All the lotuses on earth awoke and blossomed
And a jewelled umbrella opened in the sky.

The child, no equal of whom had been known,
Took seven steps in each of the directions,
And the melodious thoughts of the one supreme on earth
Echoed throughout a billion worlds.

Instantly all his father's wishes were fulfilled,
Even the gods appeared and paid homage,
"God of gods" he was called, and "Siddhartha,"
"He who Fulfills All Wishes."

Brahmins and *rishis* with the five clairvoyant powers
Prophesied: "He will be a universal emperor, or a Buddha;
But in this age of conflict there can be no such emperor,
So surely he is destined for Buddhahood."

From birth the child had perfect knowledge
Of the sixty-four forms of grammar and speech.
He was also learned in mathematics and astrology,
Yet to benefit others he entered into study.

Once while meditating under a *jambu* tree,
The shadow of the tree would not pass from him,
And *rishis* with magical powers filled the skies.
His father and five sages saw this, and bowed down.

Apprehensive, the Shakya clan plotted:
"If contented with a beautiful queen
He will become an emperor, not a mendicant."
And they counselled him to take a wife.

But the youth answered, "Attachment has faults:
Quarrels follow from it, and it is the root of sorrow.
It is to be feared as is a poisonous plant;
It is like fire or a very sharp sword."

"However, just as the *rishis* of the past
Have, though free from lust, taken wives,
So should I take a wife
And lead my subjects to the city of freedom."

"But she must be no ordinary woman.
She should be gentle and with desire for no other,
Free from vanity and conceit, true
And constant always in the ways of Dharma."

At that time a neighbouring king
Offered the hand of his daughter Yasodhara.
He planned a contest for those who would win her
And spread news of the event far and wide.

Proud Devadatta came, and with a blow killed an elephant;
But Prince Siddhartha took the elephant on his toenail
And threw it five hundred spans beyond the town.
An enormous pit formed in the place where it fell.

The gods exclaimed from a circle in the sky:
"This portends that with the strength of wisdom
He shall seize those puffed up with pride
And toss them beyond the city of samsara."

Then five hundred noble youths arrived
And entered the courtyard full of ambition.
As the competition was about to begin, the Shakyas
And thousands of spectators gathered around.

First they would contest in languages and letters,
But in the tongues of the gods, asuras and gandharvas
Siddhartha had long been thoroughly fluent,
Whereas the others did not know these even by name.

Five hundred quick-minded young men
Entered into a test of numbers,
But the Prince in the mere draw of a breath
Could count every atom of the world.

Inspired by adolescent pride the suitors
Began to wrestle one with another,
But none could bear the Prince's radiance or splendour
And on merely touching him fell to the earth.

The gods exclaimed from a circle in the sky:
"Even if all the world's strong men
Amass now to attack and destroy him,
Merely on seeing him their intentions will fail.

"With his hand he can reduce Mount Meru to dust,
And he has the power in a single moment
To destroy all the forces of darkness.
Is it a wonder he should win this small match?"

Then they offered the Prince a great bow
That his ancestors could not even bend.
Without rising from his seat but remaining crossed-legged,
With one finger he effortlessly sounded its string.

"How easily he makes the bow sing," cried the gods,
"Whilst not even rising from his seat:
A symbol that he will easily fulfil all wishes
And effortlessly crush the powers of night."

He took up the great bow, fitted an arrow
And pierced five metal sheets and seven thick trees.
The arrow travelled further still
And a well formed in the place where it fell.

"This indicates that he will sit in Vajrasana
And, fitting the bow of samadhi with arrows of wisdom,
Will penetrate without hindrance the many delusions
And reveal a precious well of the elixir of life."

When the Prince had thus gained unquestionable victory
In matches of both learning and strength
And his skill was seen by all as supreme,
The King gave him Yasodhara's hand.

Homage to Siddhartha who matured this world
Of hundreds of thousands of men and gods
By acting in accord with the worldly dharmas,
While remaining unstained by worldly ways.

But soon the gods conceived that the Prince
Had remained long enough at the side of a woman
And should manifest mahabodhi for the sake of the world.
"Therefore, you should leave the kingdom," they said.

The time came when he knew he must part,
For the Buddhas of the ten directions whispered in his ear,
"Remember the prayers you made long ago
To manifest as Buddha to benefit the world !

"You long endured hardship for the sake of the world,
So renounce your wife, your son and even your life.
For the sake of all that lives become a monk
And quickly gain the state of peerless bodhi."

Shortly thereafter while walking in the garden
He saw men in twisted states of weakness,
Men tortured by sickness, old age and death.
Disillusioned with samsara, thoughts of freedom arose.

He saw a mendicant peaceful and serene.
"A monk is praised by the wise," he thought;
"His life is happy and he attains to immortality.
For the sake of myself and others, I should follow that way."

His father came to know of his plan
And in order to prevent him from leaving the palace,
Gave him dozens of concubines enticing and skilled
And surrounded the palace with a powerful guard.

But in a dream the Prince saw himself sleeping
With the earth as his bed and the mountains his pillow,
And he saw himself fill the three worlds with light.
These and other visions came as he slept.

The next day he went to his father and announced,
"The time has come for me to go;
Did sickness, old age and death not exist,
I should remain forever; but alas, it is not so."

Yet the Shakya elders thought this unacceptable.
They surrounded the city with a profusion of guards
And placed a thousand strong men at the gate;
Such were the efforts made to keep him at home.

That midnight the sky filled with gods
And the palace was made drunk with sleep.
Chandaka came and offered him a supreme horse,
Which he mounted and flew swiftly away.

"Until I win enlightenment," he vowed,
"I shall not again enter the royal domain."
And he raced six yogana into the night
Before he dismounted and gave back the horse.

With the blade of his sword blue as a lotus
He severed his hair and tossed it to the sky.
The gods carried it to the Heaven of Thirty-Three,
And enshrined it in a golden stupa.

From Suddhavasha Heaven appeared one in saffron robes
Who exchanged his clothes for the Prince's royal garb.
These the god placed on top of his head
And flew with them as an offering to his realm.

The gods filled the sky with joyous songs:
"For the world he shaves his head and takes robes,
For the good of the world he renounces the world.
Ah, Prince Siddhartha has become a monk!"

His home was a palace born from virtue,
A mansion equalling that of a god;
But he saw it as a blazing city of hell
And left his kingdom for the homeless way.

He was like an emperor holding in his hands
Power over four continents covered by the seven jewels,
But he saw this as transient and without essence
And went by himself to a place of seclusion.

He had beautiful queens with youth and charm,
Consorts of splendour surpassing the *devi*;
But he saw them as corpses putrid and filthy
And, forsaking lust, went alone to the forest.

He walked to the banks of the Nairanjana River
And there strove again and again to reverse confusion.
For six years he submitted himself to every austerity
And dwelt in samadhis vast as the sky.

His body was reduced to skin and bone
And his very breath ceased to move.
Men and the gods thought him dead
And even his mother in heaven felt doubt.

"Ah, mother," he cried, "you need not fear.
Sun, moon and stars may fall to earth
But I will not die before my aims are fulfilled.
Be sure; see how soon I shall become a Buddha."

"But", he thought, "torturing body and mind with austerities
Is not the way to gain peerless awakening.
I must strengthen this body with ordinary food
And then carry it to the Bodhi-tree, to meditate there."

The farm girl Sujata heard these words
And with milk seven times refined drawn from a thousand cows
She made a porridge of rice and honey,
And offered it in a swastika-embellished bowl.

Nourished, his body transformed as if to polished gold
And his virtues blazed with a sublime radiance.
The brilliance of his perfections manifested as a halo
And his divine splendour shone as never before.

In order to crush delusion and to gain perfect awakening
He set out and travelled to the great Bodhi-tree.
As he walked the trees and hills bowed down toward him
And signs of auspiciousness filled heaven and earth.

All good forces of the ten directions conjoined
To contribute to this essence of full awakening.
"Ah! The fruits of virtue are inconceivable," cried the gods,
And they were transported by a joyous wonder and awe.

As the Master approached the sacred tree,
His physical aura calmed the world's pains.
Living beings, overwhelmed by joy, for a moment left delusion
And bathed in feelings of mutual love.

From the grass-cutter Swastika, the One Thus Gone
Accepted grasses fine, blue, soft and long.
Under the mighty tree he prepared himself a seat
And, entering the vajra-posture, focussed his mind.

He made a pledge as firm as Mount Meru:
"My body may parch and fall to dust,
But I will not release this posture and arise
Before perfect and supreme Buddhahood is realised."

Lights went out from the point between his eyebrows
And shook the mandala of Mara himself.
The lights flashed in ten billion world systems
And the realm of demons trembled and turned dark.

A voice deep and strong resounded in their ears:
"The son of King Suddhodana has left his kingdom
And is sitting in samadhi beneath the great Bodhi-tree.
Soon he will teach Dharma and empty the world of demons."

At that time in a dream the demon King of Maras
Saw his realm sink in darkness and confusion.
Thirty-two nightmares and bad omens came to haunt him
And he saw his followers panic and flee.

Embraced by apprehension, he cried to his forces:
"Terrifying signs and dreams I have seen
Of a monk who, should he win enlightenment,
Will certainly cause our land to be emptied.

"O four branches of my army, go out now
To that solitary mendicant seated under the tree.
Go carefully and destroy him quickly,
Do not hesitate, you who see me as king."

His forces of darkness shrieked in terror:
"But the dreams and omens advise we retreat.
A weak party is easily destroyed by one great warrior—
The sun can outshine countless fireflies!"

Yet they could not contain their anger and spite.
They emanated in every terrible form,
Took up all evil types of weapons
And gathered before the fearless hero.

Yet when the Master saw these horrific forms
He perceived them to be without an essence,
Like a dream, a mirage, an illusion—
And not a hair on his gracious body stirred.

Every bristle on the demons' bodies transformed
Into an arm clasping a hundred weapons.
They tossed these violently at the compassionate Muni
But he turned them all into delightful flowers.

A voice called, "This earth and Mount Meru could be burned,
But he with the diamond mind is invincible.
The armies of Mara could shake the three worlds,
Yet they cannot stir one hair on a Muni."

"A Muni holds no sharp or pointed weapons
And has no horses, chariots, elephants or soldiers;
Yet by himself and in a single moment
He can reverse every malignant force.

"Were the maras to manifest as a great wind,
They could rock the entire universe;
But he who is a mountain rising from an ocean of goodness
Cannot be moved from the ground of enlightenment.

"This earth could be covered by a poison
Potent enough to consume a billion worlds;
But merely a glance from a Buddha could counteract it,
For he has totally eradicated the three psychic poisons.

"A pack of jackals haunting a wilderness scatter
Into the ten directions at the roar of a lion;
Likewise the maras with their meaningless chatter
Scatter at the melodious voice of a lion amongst men.

"Mara could throw at him every stone of Mount Meru,
But these would only strengthen his celestial mansion;
And Mara could breath at him every fiery flame,
But these could only magnify his aura.

"The Muni for many uncountable aeons
Practised generosity from the depths of his heart;
Hence even the earth goddess Sthavara obeys his command."
And the forces of delusion were terrified and ran.

Then the enticing daughters of Mara appeared
And tried with the thirty-two seductive ways to attract him,
But they could not beguile him even slightly.
At the feet of the Victorious One I bow and sing praise.

When the Buddha was finally all-victorious,
Eight goddesses with sixteen graces sang his eulogy
And the gods of the Pure Abodes Heaven
In the sixteen ways ridiculed the maras.

Thus through love he conquered darkness
And by perfecting meditation gained clairvoyance.
Homage to him who at the break of dawn
Won peerless enlightenment with the vajra-like samadhi.

Without an army or weapons he defeated the enemy delusion
And with no material agent cleansed himself of karmic stains.
Unasked, he accepted personal responsibility for the world
And manifested as an unprecedented universal teacher.

Abandoning alluring wealth, a princely body and even thoughts
     of life,
He practised hundreds of profound austerities
Difficult even to believe or understand,
Thus fulfilling the essence of his sublime aspirations.

Having gained full awakening, for seven times seven days
The Muni remained under the *tarayana* tree.
The merchants Trapusa and Bhallika saw him
Ablaze with marks of perfection, and were enawed.

"Could this be Brahma?"—they asked—"Or Indra?
Or is it Vaishravana, Surya or perhaps the god Chandra?
For he wears his saffron robes resplendent as victory banners!"
And they bowed to him and offered him food.

To benefit the merchants he accepted their offering
And chanted a verse that they might know joy.
The four great kings came and each offered him a stone bowl,
Which he accepted and magically transformed into one.

Yet for some time the Muni sat unspeaking;
For he wished to generate respect for the Dharma in this realm,
He wished to demonstrate the great rarity of the teachings
And to give beings merit through requesting many times.

The gods themselves came before him:
"The very reason for which you sought enlightenment
Was to guide the world to the one-tasteness of bliss.
Therefore, to sit in silence is not right," they pleaded.

"Mankind, blind, falls from a cliff of ignorance;
Who else is there to protect them?
Arise, O great ocean of compassion,
And turn the holy Wheel of Dharma."

The Muni then arose and walked to Varanasi,
Where all universal teachers of the past had taught.
Here he himself had previously made countless offerings
And served hundreds upon hundreds of Awakened Beings.

There he sat upon a throne made of the seven gems
And for the five excellent monks and many gods
Turned the wheel of the four noble truths.
Countless listeners gained the eye of Dharma
And achieved the path to liberation.

Perfect Buddha, self-born lord of truth,
Excellent leader, peerless navigator and Dharma King,
He victorious over obstacles and mental obscuration,
To you, great patron of truth, I bow down.

One of perfected thought, fulfiller of wishes,
Omniscient possessor of ten powers, lord without delusion,
King of doctors, healer of spiritual ills,
To you, an all-good refuge, I bow down.

Teacher of living beings, supreme protector and refuge,
Light of truth, friend of the world,
Peerless field of merit poised always in samadhi,
Sage worthy of offerings and praise, to you I bow.

Never again shall imperfections stain you,
For in wisdom, love and power you are complete.
In all times and ways I prostrate myself
To you whom even to see, hear or recollect brings joy.

Through nearness to both wisdom and compassion
You abide in neither samsara nor nirvana;
Yet with wise and skilful means you demonstrated parinirvana
And manifested countless sacred relics to benefit the world.

The qualities of a Buddha are limitless as the sky;
Who is able to describe them all?
But, ah, how fortunate am I to have the karma
To be able to relate the few of which I know.

By any merits this eulogy may have,
May all living beings gain the state of Buddha;
May outer and inner hindrances be quelled,
And all harmonious conditions arise.

By the kindness of the Buddhas may all beings one day
Equal the great and wise Bodhisattvas of the past;
And may we uphold in all times, places and situations
The sacred Dharma so helpful to man.

May all beings swiftly attain the five certainties
Of One Thus Gone: a Mahayana entourage, immortality,
A pure land, the marks and signs of perfection
And perfect skill in expounding the Great Way.

By the strength of this text being composed and read,
May every place on the face of the earth
Be without sickness, poverty and war
And be filled with Dharma and omens of goodness.

May the sun of Dharma shine as bright
As it did during the life of Buddha himself;
And may the Buddhist leaders be as one family,
That the doctrine may flourish with strength and for long.

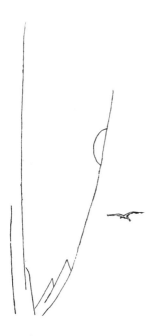

Chapter II:

Notes On Spiritual Transformation

A brief treatise on Atisha's
"Spiritual Transformation in the Mahayana Tradition"

Homage to the Buddhas and Bodhisattvas

This brief commentary to Atisha's *Spiritual Transformation in the Mahayana Tradition* will explain the following three subjects: the lineage of the *lo-jong* tradition, which is mentioned in order to show its sound sources; the power of its effects upon practitioners, which is related in order to generate respect for the tradition; and the actual substance of the jewel-like *lo-jong* teaching.

The *Root Text* itself gives the lineage:

> *This essential, nectar-like oral teaching*
> *Is the lineage of holy Ser-ling-pa.*

That is to say, from Buddha it passed in an unbroken line to Ser-ling-pa, (Tib gSer-gling-pa), "He of the Golden Isle", the illustrious master (of Sumatra) from whom Atisha himself directly received it.

As for the power of its effects upon meditators, the *Root Text* states,

> *Like a diamond sceptre, the sun, and a medicinal tree:*
> *Thus should this text and its essential points be understood;*
> *For it transforms into the bodhi-path*
> *The onslaught of today's five barbaric conditions.*

This tradition of Mahayana spiritual transformation should be known to resemble a diamond sceptre; for just as a diamond sceptre can crush rocks, mountains and so forth, this can disperse all spiritual and mundane poverty and can spontaneously fulfil all wants and needs. It is like the radiance of a tiny fragment of a diamond sceptre, which outshines that of much larger pieces of gold or any other precious metal: a partial training in it surpasses the complete path of many lesser traditions. Any aspect of this tradition is effective in destroying self-cherishing, and the tradition as a whole directly counteracts it. Thus it is likened to a cube, every side of which can be put to use, or the cube as a whole can be utilised.

The essential points of the tradition are like the sun, for they dispel mental distortions like the sun dispels darkness. A single ray of the rising sun not only clears away a proportionate degree of darkness, but also heralds the coming of the full brilliance of complete daybreak. Similarly, when one ray of the essential points of this tradition enters into the mind, it not only disperses a proportionate degree of mental distortion but also heralds a total rebirth of spiritual experience.

This tradition and its essential points should be known to resemble a medicinal tree having the power to overcome all diseases. Just as every piece of a medicinal tree—its branches, leaves, etc.—is useful to a doctor, this tradition as a whole or even any of its essential points directly cure the diseases of distortion, unknowing and grasping at a self, as well as self-cherishing, their immediate product.

In particular, Mahayana *lo-jong* uses the five degenerate conditions of this era—the viciousness of the times, the crude state of beings, the short lifespan, the superficiality of the spiritual vision of the age, and the predominance of delusion—as forces conducive to progress along the path leading to bodhi, or enlightenment.

The actual substance of the jewel-like *lo-jong* tradition is comprised of seven points: (I) The preliminary practices; (II) the actual practice: generating the two types of bodhimind; (III) transforming negative conditions into aids on the path; (IV) the doctrine of a practice for one lifetime; (V) the signs of progress; (VI) commitments of *lo-jong* practice; and (VII) general advice for Mahayana *lo-jong* practitioners.

I, THE PRELIMINARY PRACTICES

The *Root Text* states,
First train in the preliminaries.

The first of the seven essential points of *lo-jong* training is the contemplation of the five preliminary meditational subjects that ripen one's mind for the actual practice of the two types of bodhimind. These five are: (A) Guruyoga, or union with the spiritual teacher; (B) the preciousness and rarity of the freedom and opportunities afforded by human rebirth; (C) impermanence and death; (D) the karmic laws of cause and effect; and (E) the shortcomings of cyclic existence.

A. GURUYOGA

Visualise a multicoloured lotus upon your head. Seated there on sun and moon cushions is your principal spiritual guide. His form is that of Amitabha, the Buddha of Boundless Light, his body is red in colour and he has one face and two hands. His legs are crossed into the vajra posture, and his hands, which are in the gesture of meditation, support a begging bowl filled with the ambrosia of immortality. He is wearing the red robes of a monk, and his body is adorned with the thirty-two major signs and eighty minor marks of a fully enlightened being. His speech has the sixty qualities of excellence and his mind is the simultaneous wisdom understanding the infinite diversity and the profound unity of all that exists. In nature he is love, compassion and the bodhimind, and he gazes with an affectionate smile at the infinite sentient beings. He is the embodiment of all the Gurus, Meditational Deities, Buddhas and Dharma Protectors that exist.

Meditating thus, recite the following verse three times:
　　Homage to all the holy teachers,
　　Embodiments of the Buddhas,
　　In nature Holders of Diamond Knowledge,
　　The roots of the Three Jewels.

Then recite the standard verse of praise to your personal teacher, visualise making the water and sensory offerings to him, and perform either the long or short mandala offering. Generate a sense of refuge in the Guru by considering that from the present

moment until the time of your enlightenment the happiness or
suffering and the good or evil fate that you experience lie in his
hands alone. Then recite as follows:—

I take refuge in the Guru, a precious Buddha.

I take refuge in the Guru, a Buddha with Dharmakaya.

I take refuge in the Guru, a Buddha with Sambhogakaya.

I take refuge in the Guru, a Buddha with Nirmanakaya.

Recite this from the depths of your heart and the marrow of
your bones as many times as is necessary. Also recite the traditional prayer to the Lineage Gurus or do the following abbreviated prayer:—

"O precious teacher, in nature all the Buddhas, I call to you.
O precious teacher, source of the nectar-like teachings, I call
to you. O precious teacher, guide and leader of all in the three
worlds, I call to you. O precious teacher, source of refuge and
hope, I call to you.

"Grant me blessings with which I may sever all negative mental
patterns from within my being. Grant me blessings with which
I may give birth to every positive spiritual quality. Grant me
blessings with which I may quickly generate the two types of
bodhimind within my continuum. Grant me blessings with
which I may further strengthen the two types of bodhimind and
may prevent them from degenerating in this life, at death, in the
bar-do and in all future lives. Grant me blessings with which I
may be able to use all negative conditions and hindrances as
aids on the path to enlightenment."

Think like this not merely in words but with every fibre of
your spirit. Then visualise that white lights shine forth from the
crown of the Guru's head. These melt into the crown of your
head, bestow blessings of the Guru's body, and purify all physical
negativities and obscurations that you have collected since time
immemorial. Red lights radiate from his throat, bestow blessings of the Guru's speech, and purify all negativities and obscurations of speech. Blue lights then shine from his heart, melt

into your heart, bestow blessings of the Guru's mind, and purify all mental negativities and obscurations collected since beginningless time. Finally, multicoloured lights emanate from all parts of the Guru's body, melt into your body, bestow all transforming powers of his body, speech, mind, qualities and enlightened activity, and purify your obscurations, together with their seeds collected through body, speech and mind since beginningless time.

Then once more recite as above "O precious teacher, in nature all Buddhas, (*etc., until...*) my source of refuge and hope, I call to you."

The gently smiling Guru melts into light, enters your body via the crown of your head and comes to your heart, where he becomes inseparably one with your mind.

Rest for awhile in this state of *Guruyoga*, or mystical union with the spiritual teacher

B. CONTEMPLATING THE FREEDOMS AND ENDOWMENTS AFFORDED BY HUMAN REBIRTH

This will be explained under three headings: (1) recognising the freedoms and endowments; (2) contemplating the significance of having a human life-form with these qualities; and (3) contemplating the difficulty of gaining such a rebirth again.

(1) The freedoms and endowments refer to the eight freedoms and ten endowments which render life spiritually meaningful.

These eight freedoms are explained in relationship to the eight states of being in which there is no freedom for spiritual practice. The first four of these refer to non-human states: being born from the forces of negative karma and delusion in hell, as a ghost, as an animal, or as a long-lived god with no discriminating wisdom. The remaining four refer to unfavourable human states: being born as a human in an era when an enlightened being has not manifested in the world; or when, although an enlightened being has come, we happen to take birth in a remote,

distant land where the four wheels of his teachings never reach;
or, although we are born near a land where a Buddha lived and
taught, we do not possess all the normal faculties of body and
mind conducive to the study and practice of the Dharma; or
we possess all the normal faculties and live in a Dharma land,
but we live under the influence of wrong views obstructive to a
spiritual life, such as the view that actions of body, speech and
mind do not produce karmic consequences, or that there is no
state of enlightenment.

The ten endowments are comprised of five personal and five
environmental qualities. The former of these are: being born
with a human body and mind; being born in a land where the
Dharma is flourishing; having all the normal faculties of body
and mind; being free of having committed any of the five inexpi-
able deeds; and having faith and confidence in the Three Baskets
of Scriptures, a great source of spiritual knowledge. These five
are called personal endowments because they are conditions
suitable for Dharma practice that are directly connected with
the continuum of one's being.

The five environmental endowments are: being born when an
enlightened master has manifested in the world; when he has
taught the Dharma; when the Doctrine is still flourishing; when
there are realized followers of his Doctrine; and having the compassionate assistance of others, which provides a physical situa-
ation suitable for intensive Dharma practice. These five are called environmental endowments because they are conditions
suitable to Dharma practice that are directly related to a stream
of existence other that specifically one's own.

(2) If one has gained a human form possessing these freedoms and endowments, one should take its essence and reap
the benefits afforded by an auspicious situation.

The final attainment of complete Buddhahood depends upon
having a suitable life-form, a suitable environment and harmo-

nious friends. The first of these is produced by the practice
of ethical discipline, the second by the practice of generosity,
and the third by cultivating patience. Each of these practices
is best performed by a man or woman having the eight freedoms
and ten endowments. Moreover, the best ethical discipline is
the path of individual liberation, and this can only be taken
by a human being. Other forms of life are unable to generate
it. Such are the immediate benefits of having the freedoms and
endowments of a human.

Yet the ultimate benefit is even more significant. Attainment
of the state of omniscient Buddhahood must be preceeded by
an experience of the Mahayana Path of Direct Vision, and this
can be gained for the first time only by a man or woman of any
of the three continents, or by a god of the desire realm who developed along the path in a previous life as a man or woman.
No other form of life can generate an initial experience of the
Mahayana Path of Direct Vision (that is, if they had not practised as a human in a previous life). Thus a life-form which is free
from the eight states of non-leisure and possesses the ten endowments is most meaningful. One should take its essence by practising Dharma and striving for enlightenment. Moreover, as the
supreme essence to be taken is the actual attainment of the state
of perfect Buddhahood, and as the main method of accomplishing this is the cultivation of the two types of bodhimind, one
should immediately begin meditating upon them.

(3) One may think; "Granted, the attainment of a human
form having the freedoms and endowments is very meaningful,
but what need is there to practise Dharma?"

Were it not difficult to regain a human life form after death,
it perhaps would not be necessary to practise Dharma. However,
in actual fact it is very difficult to attain a human rebirth. This
is so from the point of view of both cause and nature.

The causes of human rebirth are very difficult to acquire.

Merely to gain rebirth in the higher realms of existence one must guard some discipline well, but in order to attain a life-form suitable for Dharma practice—a form with the freedoms and endowments — one must have especially strong discipline; and this is extremely rare in the present age.

In terms of nature, the number of human beings is very small in comparison to the infinitely large number of other forms of life, such as animals, insects, birds, ghosts, hell beings, and so forth. Even within the world of humans, a person with all eight freedoms and ten endowments—a suitable vessel for pure Dharma practice — is exceedingly rare. Take advantage of this valuable life you have found and extract its essence by striving for Buddhahood.

C. IMPERMANENCE AND DEATH

This involves three contemplations: (1) The certainty of death; (2) the uncertainty of the time of death; and (3) the fact that at the time of death nothing except Dharma is of value.

1. You may think: "Granted, I have found a human form with the freedoms and endowments difficult to find and, once found, most meaningful: but why should I strive to take its essence?"

Because death is inevitable. Were this not so, there perhaps would be no urgency in spiritual practice; but in actual fact it is certain that I must die. The Lord of Death definitely will come, and nothing shall be able to turn him away. There is no way to increase my lifespan, and each day its remainder becomes a day less. Even now while I am alive I find little time to practice Dharma.

The Lord of Death comes to everyone, regardless of their material status, their dwellings or the time in which they live. Nothing can prevent him from coming to me. Although I may run, I cannot run fast enough; and even armies cannot stop him. Nor are medicines, wealth or mantras able to turn him away.

There is no way to add to my life-force, and each day it uninterruptedly comes closer to death. I may live to a hundred years of age, yet each year is consumed by months, each month by days, and each day by hours. Even now much of my life has passed, and conditions of death hover over what of it remains.

Although I am now alive, I find very little time to practise Dharma. Take the example of the man who lives for a hundred years. Thoughts of Dharma rarely arise during the first decade of his life, and during the last decades he is too old and weak to practise. As for the remaining time, almost half of it is given to sleep and the other half is dedicated largely to worldly concerns such as outdoing competitors and helping friends in the wealth game, and to interruptions such as diseases and so forth. Very little remains for Dharma practice. Yet death even now is rapidly approaching. Determine to take the essence of life—to win enlightenment—before the opportunity is lost.

2. "Granted, death is inevitable. But now I am young and can give my time to outdoing enemies, protecting friends and gathering wealth and possessions, and can leave the practice of Dharma until I am old."

However, there is no certainty that you will not die before you reach old age, for on this planet the life of man has no fixed length. Many causes of death continually surround us, the causes sustaining life are fragile, and the things that support our life can easily become a cause of our death. The physical body supporting our life is delicate and can be destroyed by the mere prick of a poisonous thorn. Do not for a moment believe you have time to spare. From this very moment think only of how to extract the essence of this life having the freedoms and endowments.

3. "Granted, the time of death is uncertain; but why does this mean that I should immediately engage in the practice of the Dharma?"

Only Dharma or spiritual learning is able to benefit us after death. At death we are not able to take even one of our cherished relatives or friends with us, nor can any of our wealth or beautiful

possessions accompany us. Even our name and the very flesh
and bones which have been with us since our birth must be left
behind. This is how we must enter the path of death. At that time
all that will be of benefit is our knowledge of Dharma. From now
on, exert yourself to take the essence of Dharma by meditating
upon the two types of bodhimind.

D. THE KARMIC LAWS OF CAUSE AND EFFECT

"Granted, death is certain. But why does this mean that I
should practise Dharma?"

Because there is no other way to guarantee that death will
be followed by a state of freedom. Beings do not disappear
into a great nothingness at death; rather, they take rebirth in
accordance with the karmic forces and the psychic propensities
that they have sown within themselves during their life.

In brief, death is followed by rebirth in either a happy or a
miserable realm. When the realm is filled with misery, those
born therein must experience suffering for tremendously long
periods of time. Contemplate the sufferings of the lower realms
and strive in practices that will keep you out of them.

To quote Arya Nagarjuna:
>Day after day think about
>The hot and cold hells.
>And think about the ghosts
>Emaciated by hunger and thirst.
>Think about and observe the animals
>Who suffer in so many ways
>Due to their ignorance.
>
>Abandon the causes of such a rebirth
>And cultivate the causes of joy.
>You have now gained a precious human form,
>Do not use it as a cause of misery.
>Take heed; cut off (such causes).

As stated here by Nagarjuna, the contemplation of the miserable realms actually involves three subjects: the suffering of the hells, the suffering of animals, and the suffering of the hungry ghosts.

Contemplation of the sufferings of the hells means thinking about the nature of the hot, surrounding, cold and occasional hells.

The holy scriptures enumerate eight hot hells: (a) "Die and Die Again," in which the beings stab each other with weapons; (b) "Black Line Hell," where they draw black lines upon each other's bodies and then cut along the lines with terrible instruments; (c) "Gather and Crush," where they are gathered together and crushed by mountains shaped like goat's heads; and (d) "Hell of Shrieks," where they cry and (e) "Great Shrieks," where they wail because of the agony caused by being burned in raging fires. In (f) "Hot Hell" they are locked inside searingly hot iron houses and in (g) "Extremely Hot Hell" are roasted alive. Lastly, the beings of (h) "Ceaseless Agony" suffer unceasingly in the flames of misery.

How long are the lifespans of those born in these hells? It is said that a day and night in the life of a denizen of the hell "Die and Die Again" is equal to the five hundred year lifespan of one of the Four Great Kings, and that a day and night in the life of these kings is equal to fifty human years. A denizen of "Die and Die Again" lives 500 times the lifespan of a Great King. The lifespan of each successive hell below this doubles in length. A life in "Extremely Hot Hell" lasts for half an aeon, and that in "Ceaseless Agony" continues for a full aeon.

Even when one eventually escapes from the hot hells themselves, the four surrounding hells remain to be faced. In the first of these, "Trench of Searing Ashes," one must walk across hot coals and ashes sinking into them up to one's knees. On escaping from this hell one enters "Putrid Swamp," where one must wade up to one's waist through mud filled with worms that bore terrible holes to the very bones of one's body. Next

one enters the hell "Forest of Trees with Razor Leaves," where one is cut to pieces by sword-like leaves that are attracted to one's body like iron filings to a magnet. Finally one enters "Desolation River," a boiling river with cliffs on both sides to prevent escape, in which one is tossed and churned unceasingly.

The sufferings in these hells are indeed terrible and of tremendous duration. Should they fall upon us, we would find them most difficult to bear. For example, most of us at the moment would have difficulty to place our hands in hot coals merely for a day.

It is not impossible that we ourselves will be reborn in one of these hells. The forces of negativity are strong, and the evil karmas collected by us since beginningless time certainly have not all ripened yet. Nor is there much possibility that we have yet counteracted them all with the meditative opponents. Many remain to be faced. In future we should avoid all evil and negativity, the causes of rebirth in hell, and should strive to practise Dharma and to live in goodness, the causes of a happy rebirth.

Eight Cold Hells are enumerated: (a) "Hell of Blisters," (b) "Bursting Blisters," (c) "Groaningly Cold Hell," (d) "Terribly Cold Hell," (e) "Frozen Face Hell," (f) "Body Cracking Open like an Utpala," (g) "Body Cracking Open like a Lotus," and (h) "The Great Dark, Cold Hell Deep under the Ice."

How long is the lifespan of those born therein? Were there to be eighty warehouses filled with sesame seeds, and were we to remove one seed every hundred years until all the seeds were gone, the time expired would equal the lifespan in the "Hell of Blisters." The lifespan in each successive hell under this is multiplied by twenty. Thus the unbearable suffering of each hell must be experienced for an exceedingly long duration of time. We would find such an incarnation very difficult to endure. At present we find it painful to stay outside naked in the middle of winter for even a few hours. Abandon negativity, the cause of rebirth in the cold hells, and strive to practise Dharma and to cultivate goodness, the causes of joy.

The Occasional Hells are said to be located near the mighty oceans and in the great deserts. The intensity of the suffering experienced in them is described by Nagarjuna in his *Friendly Letter* :

Being struck continuously for a day
By three hundred terrible spears
Is nothing compared to a day in these hells.
No image can convey the experience.

Once more I urge you: abandon negativity, the cause of lower rebirth, and strive to produce the causes of joy.

The animal realm is also filled with misery. Animals suffer in many ways, such as exposure to the elements, domestication, eating one another and so forth. The shortest lifespan of an animal (insect, fish, bird, etc.) is not measurable, for many die even while they are being born; but it is said that certain types of animals live for an aeon. Should we take rebirth in such a realm, we would find life unendurable. At present we find even the tiny sting of a bee hard to take. Abandon evil and negativity, the causes of rebirth in the animal realm; and strive to produce the causes of joy.

Usually it is said that there are thirty-six species of hungry ghosts; but these are subsumed under three categories: ghosts with internal problems, external problems and problems in obtaining food and drink.

Ghosts are said to live for five hundred years, each day of which equals a month in human reckoning. Thus their sufferings must be endured for long. Who would desire to fall into such a world? At present we can hardly bear going even a few days without food or drink. Yet within ourselves we carry many karmic seeds for rebirth as a ghost, and there is no certainty that these will not ripen at the time of death. We should there- fore strive to eliminate from within our mindstreams all causes of a lower rebirth, and should try to cultivate the causes of happiness.

What exactly are the methods of gaining freedom from the lower realms and of attaining the states of lasting joy? These are twofold: (1) taking refuge in the Three Jewels; and then (2) gaining an understanding of and living in accordance with the karmic laws of cause and effect.

1. TAKING REFUGE

1. Refuge is dealt with under four headings: (a) the reasons for taking refuge; (b) the objects of refuge; (c) how to take refuge; and (d) the precepts of refuge.

(a) The reasons for taking refuge are twofold: one fears the experience of suffering characteristic of lower forms of life; and one realises that the Three Jewels have the power to help one to transcend them.

(b) There are three objects of refuge: the Buddhas, who have eliminated all faults and attained to every excellence; the Dharma taught by them, or the path to Buddhahood; and the Sangha, or the experienced practitioners who help us along the way.

As the text *Twenty Pledges* states,
> Freedom seekers turn for refuge
> To the Buddha, Dharma and Sangha.

You may ask: "Why is Buddha a more reliable object of refuge than, for instance, a god? Because a reliable object of refuge should himself be above every shortcoming, should be perfectly wise in showing others how to overcome their own shortcomings, should have the great compassion which is above liking those who worship and respect him and disliking those who do not do so, and also should be above thinking in terms of who is and who is not beneficial to him. A Buddha by definition has perfected all of these qualities, whereas the gods have not completely perfected any.

If the Buddha is a reliable object of refuge, the Dharma taught by him must be reliable, for he gained his state of enlightenment solely by practicing the Dharma that he later taught. For the same reasons the Sangha can be regarded as worthy, for the Sangha by definition implies meditators accomplished in the practise of Dharma.

(c) How to take refuge is explained under four headings: (1) taking refuge with an understanding of the greatness of the Three Jewels; (ii) taking refuge with an understanding of the uniqueness of the three; (iii) the refuge formula; and (iv) not mistaking the refuge objects.

(i) In order to take refuge in the Buddhas, Dharma and Sangha we must first gain an appreciation of their significance and efficacy. This is generated by being mindful of their qualities.

To be mindful of the greatness of the Buddhas means to recollect constantly their qualities of body, speech, mind and activity.

The body of a Buddha is adorned by the thiry-two major signs and the eighty minor marks of perfection. His speech is such that if all the beings on earth simultaneously were to ask him a different question he could answer with one statement, and all would hear the reply in their own terms and would find the statement to be a perfect response to their question. His mind possesses wisdom that sees all things—both relative and ultimate—as clearly as a piece of transparent fruit held in the palm of the hand. It possesses compassion so strong that, just as sentient beings are powered solely by the force of delusion, a Buddha is motivated purely by great compassion. His consciousness flows in an unbroken stream with the thought to free the sentient beings from suffering.

As for the activities of a Buddha's body, speech and mind, they effortlessly and spontaneously manifest in an unbroken stream whenever and wherever sentient beings are sufficiently ripe to be benefitted,

The greatness of a Buddha is the strongest proof of the excellence of the Dharma; for the Buddha, who possessed these extraordinary qualities, achieved his exalted state solely through practice of the scriptural and insight Dharmas that he later expounded.

Similarly, if we appreciate the Dharma we should also appreciate the Sangha; for the Sangha are none other than the advanced practitioners of the Dharma.

(ii) Taking refuge with an understanding of the unique qualities of each of the Three Jewels means that one should have a clear understanding of what differentiates the Three Jewels from one another.

(iii) The refuge formula is as follows: "I turn for refuge to Buddha, the teacher; to Dharma, the actual refuge; and to the Sangha, the friends on the way."

(iv) Not mistaking the refuge objects means that at the time of refuge one should have a clear understanding of the defining characteristics, qualities and shortcomings of the various non-Buddhist founders, doctrines, and lineages of practitioners, and how these compare with the founder, doctrines and lineages of practitioners of the Buddhist tradition. To be a Buddhist, one should feel a strong karmic preference for the latter system over the former.

(d) The precepts of refuge are twofold: (i) the specific precepts of the Three Jewels; and (ii) the general refuge precepts.

(i) The specific precepts of refuge in the Three Jewels are of two types: those dealing with things to be avoided and those with things to be accomplished.

Refuge in Buddha specifically means that one should avoid relying upon any of the worldly gods, such as Ishvara or Vishnu, for anything but temporary assistance. Refuge in the Dharma means that one should avoid harming any living being. And Refuge in the Sangha entails that one should avoid spending time with those who hinder one's Dharma practice

From the point of view of things to be accomplished, the specific precept of Refuge in Buddha is to regard all images of Buddha as being embodiments of Buddha himself, and not to concern oneself with the qualities or flaws of the craftmanship of the image. Refuge in the Dharma means that one should consider every single verse of the scriptures to be the essence of all Dharma and should venerate it accordingly. Finally, refuge in the Sangha entails that one should regard even those monks who wear the robes solely externally as being the true sangha.

(ii) As for the general precepts of refuge, generate an understanding of the unique nature and excellent qualities of each of the Three Jewels, constantly maintain an awareness of your refuge in them and remember their beneficial effects upon your spiritual life. Make offerings to them at all times, such as offering them the first portion of everything that you eat or drink. Also, with constant mindfulness of the sacred nature of the Three Jewels, guide others in refuge to the best of your ability. Before commencing any activity, direct the work into an offering to the Three Jewels and make prayers that your efforts may bring you realisation of the inner meaning of refuge, for the sake of all sentient beings. Do not do anything without first directing the energy in this way. Three times each day and three times each night recite the refuge formula while recollecting the beneficial effects of refuge. Lastly, do not forsake refuge even in jest or to save your life.

What are the beneficial effects of having taken refuge in the Three Jewels? One is turned toward the spiritual path and is made into a vessel suitable for the various Dharmic disciplines. All of one's negativities accumulated since beginingless time are made thin and are caused to fade away. One gains a vast reservoir of spiritual energy and after death will not be prone to lower rebirth. Neither men nor ghosts will be able to harm one, all of one's wishes will become actuality and one will be able to quickly gain the stage of perfect enlightenment.

Remember these advantages and meditate on taking refuge three times daily and three times at night.

2. GAINING AN UNDERSTANDING OF KARMIC LAW

This entails first recognising the nature of negative action, or, to be more particular, the ten types of negative deeds of body, speech and mind. (Three of these are of the body: killing, stealing and abuse of the sexual capacity ; four are of speech: lying, slander, harsh words and meaningless talk; and three are of the mind: attachment, ill-will and holding wrong views.)

The ripening effects of these deeds, in terms of how they affect us after death, is that a grossly evil karma leads to rebirth in hell, a medium evil leads to rebirth as a ghost, and a minor evil results in rebirth as an animal.

The effect similar to the cause in the case of, for example, killing, is that even should one find a human rebirth one will die by being killed at an early age. In the case of stealing, one will have problems with finances and possessions in future lives.

The effect on our environment, e.g., in the case of killing, is that one will be reborn in a remote, barren and harsh land. Or, as a result of stealing, countless damages will fall upon one's property.

The nature of the ten positive actions is the opposite of their negative counterparts. For example, the ripening effect of a strongly positive karma is rebirth as a god in the upper heavens; of a karma of medium virtue is rebirth as a god in the heavens of sensory pleasures; and of a deed of minor virtue is rebirth as an ordinary human having little spiritual interest.

The effect similar to the cause of, for example, avoiding killing, is that we gain a long life. Similarly, by not taking what is not given we are reborn in circumstances blessed with the presence of physical necessities.

The effect on our environment of, for instance, protecting life and avoiding killing, is that we are reborn into a highly civilised country. By avoiding stealing we never again (in future lives) have problems with our own possessions and properties.

Abandon negative karma, the cause of your own downfall, and cultivate the causes of happiness within your continuum.

E. THE SHORTCOMINGS OF CYCLIC EXISTENCE

You may think: "Yes, I will abandon evil, the cause of suffering and of rebirth in the lower realms, and will practise virtue, the cause of happiness and a higher rebirth; and thus I will gain rebirth as a man or god, which is a sufficient attainment." However, it is not sufficient, for the entirety of cyclic existence is by nature suffering.

Men have the sufferings of birth, sickness, old age, death, encountering the unpleasant, losing what is pleasing to them, not getting all that they strive for, and so forth. They experience all the sufferings and frustrations that come with having imperfect mental, physical and emotional bases.

The gods of the Sensuous Heavens know tremendous suffering when the five certain signs and five minor omens portending their death appear. As their energies wane, they are filled with unbearable jealously at the splendour of the younger gods. Throughout their lives they suffer from continual competition with the other gods, and the weaker are driven into exile by the stronger and are forced to live alone.

The antigods have the sufferings of constantly fighting with one another and of warring with the higher gods. Many are their pains from the cutting of limbs, and from witnessing their near and dear ones die in battle.

Gods of the highest heavens have no immediate sufferings, but they have no possibility to regenerate their spiritual energies. When the stabilised karma that threw them to their rebirth has expired, again they must fall to the lower realms and must experience the gross sufferings; just as an arrow shot into the sky is sure to return to earth sooner or later.

Hence it is said that no matter what realm of cyclic existence one is reborn into, it is a place of suffering; no matter with whom one travels, one is accompanied only by suffering; and no matter what possessions one may own, they will not take one beyond the claws of suffering. Thus we should strive to attain the state of nirvana, which has abandoned all suffering.

The methods for attaining nirvana are: taking refuge in the Three Supreme Jewels; meditating upon the twelve links of interdependent origination both in terms of how they evolve and how they are to be reversed upon themselves; meditating upon the understanding of egolessness, that cuts off ego-grasping, the root of cyclic existence; and, in brief the practice of the three higher trainings: ethical discipline, meditative concentration and wisdom.

II. THE ACTUAL PRACTICE: GENERATING THE TWO TYPES
OF BODHIMIND.

The actual substance of the *lo-jong* training is the cultivation
of the two types of bodhimind: (A) the conventional bodhimind,
and (B) the ultimate bodhimind.

(A) CULTIVATING THE CONVENTIONAL BODHIMIND.

Accomplishment of the three higher trainings results in personal
nirvana; yet this is not a sufficient spiritual attainment. The
two types of nirvana-attainers, that is, the Sravaka Arhants and
Pratyekabuddhas, do in fact abide in nirvana; but they have
completed merely a fraction of the abandonments and insights
concommitant with full enlightenment. Consequently, they cannot
be said to have fully achieved ultimate benefit for either themselves or others. Sooner or later they must turn to the path leading
to Buddhahood, the state of full enlightenment that has completed all abandonments and insights. One day a Buddha will send
them rays of light from his inspiring presence, and will admonish
them to enter the Mahayana path and become Buddhas them-

selves. It would be much wiser to aim for full Buddhahood from the very beginning of one's practice; and to take up its cause, which is the Mahayana Vehicle.

What, then, is the door leading to the Mahayana? It is nothing other than the Mahayana attitude, the bodhimind. One may possess tremendous meditative concentration and wisdom, yet if one's mindstream is not blended with the bodhimind one's feet are not on the Mahayana path. Alternatively, even if one has neither samadhi nor wisdom but has the bodhimind, one stands firmly on the Mahayana. A person is a Mayahanist only if he has the bodhimind. Whether or not one progresses or regresses along the Mahayana path depends solely upon whether or not one's bodhimind increases or degenerates. Therefore those who aspire to accomplish the Mahayana ideal must take up the practice of the bodhimind.

How is this to be done? There are two ways: (A) developing the bodhimind by means of the method called "Six Causes and One Result"; and (B) developing it by means of the method called "Exchanging Self-Awareness for Awareness of Others."

(A) THE METHOD CALLED "SIX CAUSES AND ONE RESULT"

Begin by generating a recognition (1) of all beings as having been your mother in a past life and (2) of the infinite kindness of the mother. From this arises (3) a wish to repay the sentient beings for their kindness. This wish transforms into (4) the love that wishes to help maintain universal happiness; and (5) the compassion that wishes to separate all beings from suffering and frustration. From this comes (6) the high resolve of universal responsibility, which produces (7) the bodhimind itself. Finally, on the basis of the bodhimind the state of Buddhahood is eventually attained.

(1) Recognising all sentient beings as having once been one's mother.

There is no form of life that we have not taken in one of our infinite lives since beginningless time; nor is there a realm into which we have not taken birth. There is no sentient being we have not known again and again, and who has not been our father, mother, teacher and student; for cyclic existence is without a beginning, and we have known birth, life and death countless billions of times.

(2) Recognising the infinite kindness of the mother sentient beings.

It is generally considered most easy to gain experience of this point by meditating upon the kindness of one's own mother. Visualise your mother sitting before you and imagine that she has been your mother in all your lives since beginningless time. Again and again she has been your mother, and each time she has been very beneficial to you and has protected you from many harms. Specifically, even in this life she has carried you in her womb for many months. After you were born she picked you up and held you to her flesh to give you her warmth. Not minding that you looked like nothing more than a fuzzy red worm, she gently took you in her hands, placed you to her breasts and fed you her own milk. She cleaned the mucus and excrement from your body and cared for you in countless ways. As you grew she gave you food and drink with which to keep away hunger and thirst, and when the cold winds blew she covered you with warm clothing. In times of poverty she shared her wealth with you without the slightest remorse at the loss to herself. She did not give you merely what she did not require herself, nor what she acquired easily. Her service to you was a physical sacrifice to herself and she worked for you even in blindness to her own pleasure or pain and loss or gain. If you became ill she felt as though ill herself, and she would rather die than to permit death to come to you. In every possible way she strove to keep you from misery. In particular, she performed the great kindness of giving you this human body which has enabled you to meet with the Dharma and to embark upon a spiritual path.

Having gained experience in the above contemplation, meditate upon the kindness of your father, relatives, friends, and even enemies, all of whom have been your mother again and again. Increase the scope of the meditation until eventually all sentient beings are included.

(3) The wish to repay the sentient beings.

Perhaps at the moment you cannot recognise as a mother anyone but your mother of this life, for, passing from life to death and to rebirth, your memory may have been weakened. But all have been your mother again and again, and each time they have shown you the kindness of protecting you from harm and giving you all the benefits of life. To ignore the tremendous kindness that they have shown you and to work for the liberation of yourself alone would be an unequalled shame. You should think instead of how to repay them.

How can you repay them? Well, from the very beginning of beginningless time they have been wandering throughout cyclic existence and undoubtedly will have experienced every form of sensual pleasure; but sensual pleasure is deceptive and does not last for long. You should aim at repaying them with the extraordinary pleasure that is beyond all sorrow: with the bliss of nirvana itself.

(4) Meditation upon the beautiful mind of love.

Visualise the sentient beings who are without happiness. Determine to place them in joy. Think, "May they be happy."

(5) Meditation upon Compassion.

Visualise the sentient beings who have sufferings. Determine
to free them from it. Think, "May they be freed from suffering."

(6) Meditation upon the extraordinary attitude.

Visualise the sentient beings who are impoverished of happiness and who are tortured by misery. Think, "May I myself
place them in peerless happiness and free them from their misery
forever."

(7) Meditation upon the bodhimind itself.

How can you fulfil the needs of all the sentient beings? At
present you cannot ultimately benefit even one of them, let
alone all. Moreover, you have not even really fulfilled all your
own spiritual needs, so speaking of fulfilling those of others
is total nonsense. Any work for the benefit of others must
begin by working on yourself. Nobody but a fully enlightened
being can really benefit others, so the first task in working for
the world is to attain Buddhahood yourself. Only this will ultimately benefit the beings.

B. EXCHANGING SELF-AWARENESS FOR AWARENESS OF
   OTHERS

This has two phases: (1) transforming the mind in terms of its
attitude toward others; and (2) transforming it in terms of its
attitude toward enlightenment.

(1) The first of these is effected in two ways: (a) exchanging
self-awareness for awareness of others by contemplating the
advantages of doing so and the disadvantages of not; and (b)
the actual technique for transforming the mind in its attitude
toward others.

(a) The *Root Text* states:

   Place all the blame on one point.

Exchanging self-awareness for the awareness of others does
not mean that we should pretend that we are someone else,

nor that our eyes or nose belong to someone else. It means relinquishing the mind which cherishes oneself and cultivating attitudes which appreciate others.

This practice is both beneficial and essential, for self-cherishing is the very source of all spiritual faults, whereas the cherishing of others is the source of all good qualities.

As Shantideva states in *A Guide to the Bodhisattva's Way of Life*,

> All the happiness that exists
> Arises from wishing joy for others,
> And all the misery that exists
> Arises from wishing happiness for oneself alone.
>
> What more need be said?
> The spiritually immature think of themselves alone,
> The Buddhas think only of others.
> Look at the difference between the two!

Relinquish self-cherishing and replace it with empathy toward others. Whenever anyone harms you or creates hindrances for your desired goals, do not blame them. Blame only your own self-cherishing. From beginningless time we have held the self-cherishing attitude, and its influence has repeatedly caused us to create negative karma through unskillful actions of body, speech and mind, thus resulting in our present experience of suffering. Even now we rely upon the self-cherishing attitude, bringing countless frustrations and problems upon ourselves again and again. Place all blame upon the real enemy, the self-cherishing attitude.

The *Root Text* then states:
Meditate upon all as being kind.

Over the countless aeons since beginningless time every sentient being has been a mother to us again and again. On each occasion they have shown us the kindness of benefitting us in many ways and protecting us against harms. We should think only about how to benefit them and to mitigate their suffering.

In brief, we immediately and directly benefit them by making them happy and we lay the seeds of future benefits for them by encouraging them in goodness. Try therefore to inspire both happiness and goodness within others.

On the other hand, we directly harm someone by giving him misery, and by encouraging him in evil we lay the seeds of his future harm. Thus we should try to free beings from misery and evil.

In order to meditate upon exchanging self-awareness for awareness of others we must first meditate upon the equality of oneself and others.

Just as I myself wish to produce happiness for myself and wish to destroy my own sufferings and frustrations, so do all beings wish happiness for themselves and wish to rid themselves of misery. I should also help them to find happiness and become free from suffering.

Why? From an objective point of view their wish for happiness and their desire to avoid misery in every way equals my own. And from a personal perspective, they have all been my mother again and again and have greatly helped me and sheltered me from harm. Their kindness has indeed been very great and I should remember it always.

To think that we should not try to relieve them of suffering merely because it is not our own problem is as shortsighted as to think that our hand need not pull out a thorn that has pierced our foot. The thorn is not harming the hand, so why should the hand do anything to help?

(b) The actual technique for transforming the mind in its attitude toward others is as follows: Once progress in the above meditation upon exchanging self-awareness for awareness of others has been gained, we should engage in the meditation known as "giving and taking." The *Root Text* states,

Practise interwoven giving and taking.

The next line of the *Root Text* explains the sequences of the practice:

Begin the taking with yourself.

What this means is that whenever we become sick or afflicted with suffering we should meditate that the experience is actually a conducive field in which to eliminate the negative karma that otherwise would result in our suffering next week, next month, next year, next lifetime, or in some future life. Contemplate that the practice of *lo-jong* done in conjunction with the specific disease or pain results in liberation from the sufferings that you would otherwise have to face next week, next month, next year, next lifetime or whenever.

Then visualise your mother sitting before you. Remember how she helped you and sheltered you from harm not only in this life but many times since beginningless existence. Specifically, even in this life she has carried you in her womb for many months; and when you were born she picked you up and held you to her flesh to give you her warmth, placed you on her breasts to feed you, cleaned the mucus and excrement from your body, and cared for you in countless ways. As you grew old she gave you food and drink with which to keep away hunger and thirst, and when the cold winds blew she covered you with warm clothing. Of particular significance, she performed the great kindness of giving you this human body which has enabled you to meditate upon the Mahayana *lo-jong* tradition. You should repay her kindness by meditating upon "giving and taking," using her as the object of concentration.

How is this done? As you inhale, meditate that your incoming breath cuts off all her sufferings as though with a knife. These take the form of a black cloud and are inhaled into your body They come to your heart and destroy your self-cherishing. Contemplate that all her mental obscurations and present and future sufferings are thus eliminated, and that she is moved toward Buddhahood.

Next visualise that all your goodness and happiness are cut off from your heart by your exhaling breath as though by a knife. This takes the form of a white cloud, leaves your body as you exhale, and enters your mother's heart. Contemplate that she thus gains all goodness and happiness.

Why does one practise "giving and taking" from the heart? Because the heart is the deepest seat of the self-cherishing attitude. Through concentrating our bodhimind meditation at the heart we attack self-cherishing with its direct opponent on its own ground.

When familiarity with the above meditation has been gained, apply the technique in a similar manner toward your father, relatives, friends, neighbours and enemies. Apply it to all the beings of this continent, then all beings of the four continents, the beings of the hells, the ghost realms, the animals, gods, anti-gods and all forms of life. Finally, apply it to Sravaka Arhants, Pratyekabuddhas, and even to Bodhisattvas of the tenth level and below; for Sravaka Arhants and Pratyekabuddhas have not surmounted the obscurations to omniscience, and even a Bodhisattva of the tenth level has not gained freedom from the very subtle stains of obscuration. Do not, however, meditate upon taking the faults of the Buddhas or of your Root Guru; for the Buddhas have no faults to be taken, and you should always meditate that your Guru is in fact a perfect Buddha and should not think that he has any shortcomings. Even if it seems to you that he has subtle faults, such as old age, recognise this to be a sign of your own impure perception and rest in the conviction that your Guru is in fact a perfect Buddha.

Usually you should visualise that you are taking on the suffering and negative karma of others, but sometimes it is permissible to visualise taking on their lust, anger or so forth. Similarly, usually you should visualise giving the sentient beings your body, possessions and virtues of the past, present and future; but occasionally you can meditate on giving specific things such as a cooling rain to the hot hells, warmth to the cold hells, food and drink to the hungry ghosts and so forth.

It is said to be inappropriate to visualise giving away the bodies of your past lives, for they are already dead; and also to give the bodies of your future lives is inappropriate, for they have not yet been created. Perhaps you will think this means that to visualise giving away past and future virtues is also invalid, for those of the past are also now gone and those of the future are as of yet uncreated. This comparison does not work. Even at the moment we are carrying the karmic seeds of all our past virtues within our mindstream, and thus to visualise giving them away is reasonable. On the other hand, all our past and present negative karmas of body, speech and mind live on as karmic seeds within us, and as it is these that ultimately will cause any future suffering we may have, to visualise taking on future suffering now is also reasonable. Similarly, all future goodness is based upon and born from the positive karmic potentialities that we now bear within us, so meditating upon giving away future goodness is also valid.

When you become somewhat proficient in this meditation of "giving and taking," the *Root Text* advises,

> *Ride upon the moving breath.*

How is this done? Beginning with you mother and eventually including all living beings, visualise that, as you inhale, the non-virtue and suffering of others comes from them to your heart in the form of a black mist. Consider that your mother and the other beings are thus freed from sufferings and negativities.

As you exhale, visualise that all your goodness and happiness take the form of white cloud-like clusters. This, together with the expelled air, leaves via your nostrils and proceeds to the heart of your mother and the others. Consider that they attain to every goodness and joy, and that they ascend to the state of perfect Buddhahood.

After you have meditated like this with your mother as the subject, apply the technique to relatives, friends and even enemies. Eventually take all sentient beings of the six realms for this ride upon the incoming and outgoing breath.

(2) Transforming the mind in terms of its attitude toward enlightenment involves two trainings: (a) the meditation to develop the wishing bodhimind, and (b) the meditation to develop the actual bodhimind.

(a) The fundamental importance of generating the wishing bodhimind is stated clearly in many sutras,

> Through familiarity with the wishing bodhimind—
> The altruistic thought to gain full Buddhahood—
> One goes to the end of cyclic existence.
> Thus its value is immeasurable.

Transforming the mind in terms of its attitude toward en-

lightenment by means of meditation upon the wishing bodhimind begins by asking yourself: "Granted, I would like to benefit the countless sentient beings; but do I actually have the
power to do so at the moment?" You should realise that in your
present condition not only do you not have power to benefit
them all, in fact you don't have power to benefit even one of
them. Not to mention others, you don't have power to benefit
even yourself. Even universal emperors, Sravaka Arhants or
Pratyekabuddhas, having completed merely a fraction of the
abandonments and insights, cannot fulfil the ultimate needs of
the sentient beings. Only someone who is completely enlightened can do so; for a single light-ray, miracle or verse of teaching
given by a fully enlightened being has the capacity to place
endless sentient beings upon the paths leading to spiritual maturity and freedom. If I wish to ultimately benefit sentient beings,
and because nobody except a fully enlightened being can effectively do so, I should aspire to attain full enlightenment for the
sake of all that lives. This aspiration is the wishing bodhimind, and it should be developed, reinforced and protected
by guarding the precepts of the enlightened attitude.

When the wishing bodhimind has reached a certain stability
one should meditate upon the actual bodhimind, which is the
bodhimind that actually engages in the deeds and practices which
produce realisation of enlightenment.

B. CULTIVATING THE ULTIMATE BODHIMIND.

The *Root Text* states,
> *When he attains proficiency,*
> *Teach him the secret.*

When the disciple has gained stability in the meditations upon conventional bodhimind, he should be taught how to meditate upon emptiness, the nature of reality not known to those who expound inherent existence.

How is this done? The *Root Text* states,
> *Consider all dharmas*
> *To be like a dream.*

Although all the infinite dharmas that exist, such as mountains, trees, etc., have no existence whatsoever, they appear to be truly existent. Meditate again and again on their illusive, dream-like quality.

Perhaps you will think, "I agree that the objects of perception are not truly existent, but surely the mind which perceives them has existence."

However, the *Root Text* states,
> *Examine the nature of the unborn mind.*

That which perceives is by true nature unproduced. To examine the nature of this unborn, unproduced awareness means to meditate upon the void nature of the mind.

The mind is said to be unborn, for it is produced neither from itself, nor from anything else, nor from both self and another, nor without a cause.

Some people see that the mind which grasps at the true existence of objects and consciousness itself has no true existence; yet they believe that the wisdom opposing (grasping) by per-

ceiving the non-true nature of objects and consciousness does truly exist. The *Root Text* states,
> *The opponent itself (is free) on its own ground.*

That is to say, the wisdom which opposes grasping at true existence itself has no true existence. By meditating upon the non-true existence of objects and consciousness, we also become free from grasping at the true existence of the opponent to grasping; for there is nothing which is not included in the two-fold category of objects (of consciousness) and consciousness itself. The wisdom of non-true existence is but a highly developed aspect of consciousness.

You may ask: "Well then, if objects, consciousness, things to be abandoned, opponents to delusion, and so forth all are non-existent, what path remains to be meditated upon?"

The *Root Text* states,
> *Place the essence of the path*
> *In the state of the foundation of all."*

The essence of practice should be unwaveringly fixed on the state of emptiness, the foundation of all.

Emptiness is called "the foundation of all" because it is the basis for both samsara and nirvana. By not understanding emptiness we wander in samsara; and by understanding empti-ness we attain freedom from samsara.

Meditate formally upon emptiness in this way several times each day. As for the post-meditation period, the *Root Text* states,
> *Practise on the three objects,*
> *Three poisons and*
> *Three roots of virtue.*
> *This in brief is the oral precept*
> *For the post-meditation period.*

After meditation sessions our awareness of emptiness is not very strong and consequently when we see beautiful people or things the mind of attachment arises. But just as this happens to us, it also happens to the infinite sentient beings when they see beautiful objects. Therefore, whenever attachment arises within you, contemplate that you are taking upon yourself all the attachments of the infinite sentient beings. Think, "Through my taking on all their attachments, may they all gain the virtuous root of non-attachment." Likewise, when you see disagreeable objects or people and aversion arises within you, consider that aversion similarly arises within the infinite sentient beings when they encounter disagreeable objects, and think that through your aversion you are taking upon yourself all of theirs. Meditate, "By my doing this, may they all gain the virtuous root of non-aversion."

Lastly, when I encounter things toward which I feel only apathy and ignorance, I should consider that, just as an object that is neither pleasant nor unpleasant to me stirs no emotion other than a vague ignorance in me, similar objects affect all other sentient beings in the same way. Consequently, I will use this experience I am now having to take upon myself the apathy and ignorance of all the world. May all the sentient beings thus gain the virtuous root of non-ignorance." Meditate purely and intensely in this way.

The *Root Text* then states,
>   *In order to remember this,*
>   *Recite it in words*
>   *Throughout all activities.*

Whether you are walking, sitting, or doing any activity whatsoever, constantly say to yourself, "May the sufferings and faults of all the living beings ripen upon me, and may any goodness or happiness that I may possess ripen upon them." Also, in all activities—walking, sitting, talking, etc.—think only of how you can take the essence of the opportunities afforded by human life, that the supreme way to do this is by attaining Buddhahood, and that one of the most effective means of actualising Buddhahood is through practising the meditation 'giving and taking.' Bear this constantly in mind and incessantly recite to yourself, "May all goodness and joy be dedicated to the other sentient beings, and may all their trials ripen upon me."

III. TRANSFORMING NEGATIVE CONDITIONS INTO AIDS ON THE PATH.

The *Root Text* states:
When the world and its beings are evil,
Transform the negative conditions
Into aids on the path to enlightenment.

The power of evil occasionally manifests and difficult experiences arise because of unsuitable physical conditions and aggressive or thoughtless sentient beings. These experiences should be transformed into aids on the path to enlightenment. This is to be done in two ways: (A) meditation upon the bodhimind; and (B) the activities of accumulating creative energy and purifying one's mindstream.

A. TRANSFORMING NEGATIVITIES THROUGH THE BODHIMIND

Meditation upon the bodhimind in both its conventional and ultimate natures is the most effective means of transforming negative conditions into spiritual aids. The following lines of the *Root Text* describe how to apply the conventional bodhimind in this way,

> *Place all the blame upon one thing alone*
> *And meditate on kindness for all.*

Whenever undesirable experiences arise, do not blame anyone or anything else. Place the blame directly upon the self-cherishing attitude, and meditate upon the kindness of whoever is giving you this problem. Take the non-virtue and suffering upon yourself and surrender your happiness and goodness to them.

Especially, whenever men or spirits harm you, remember that in many previous lives they have been your mother. On those occasions they gave no thought to their own happiness, pain or social standing, but, thinking only of how to protect and nourish you, they experienced much misery on your behalf. These sentient beings are now disturbing you not out of true malice but only because they are overpowered by delusion and have no recognition of your previous relationships. Moreover, it is because of your own negative karma that they are harming you, for if you had no karmic faults you would not be able to be affected by them. By harming you they are planting within themselves karmic seeds for their own future suffering, so you are serving as a condition for their negative activity and as a cause of their creating future sorrow for themselves. Merely by being a victim of their negativity you are doing them a greater harm than they are doing to you. How pathetic! Meditate upon taking their suffering and evil karma upon yourself and on giving them happiness and virtue. Whenever men or animals harm you, think only of how you can benefit them in return. Even when there is nothing you can actually do to benefit them, at least think, "May this harmful being be forever free from suffering. May he/she have happiness and quickly attain to full and perfect enlightenment."

Should gods or evil spirits try to harm you, remember that many times throughout beginningless cyclic existence you have eaten their flesh and blood. Imagine making them an offering of your own flesh and blood as a token repayment. Visualise the god or spirit before you and say to it, "I cut open this body of mine with the scapel of my intellect and offer you its flesh and blood. Please take what you would." Contemplate that he takes it and that it satiates his hunger and thirst, calms his suffering and fills him with transcendental great bliss of body and mind. This practice is effective in pacifying all types of gods, spirits, ghosts and demons.

Negative conditions can also be transformed into aids on the path through meditation upon the ultimate bodhimind.

The *Root Text* states,
   Meditate that all confused appearances
   Are the four Buddha-kayas.
   The best guardian is emptiness.

No matter what types of suffering or what problems arise— mental frustration or perhaps inner or outer harms—consider that they are only deluded appearances. In actuality they are not even slightly truly existent. They exist conventionally only in the manner of one's being drowned or burned in a dream. Just as a sleeping man believes the objects of his dream to be real, so we now grasp at what appears to us. However, neither delusion nor suffering have true existence. They are the Unborn Truth Body (*Skt. Dharmakaya*) because from the beginning they have never been created. They are the Undying Beatific Body (*Skt. Sambhogakaya*) because, not being created, they have no destruction. They are the Unabiding Emanation Body (*Skt. Nirmanakaya*) for, having neither creation nor destruction, they cannot possibly abide. And they are the Indivisible Essence Body (*Skt. Svabhavakaya*) because they are of the above three inseperable natures. Such is the precept called "Introduction to the Four Kayas." The foremost guardian of this precept is meditation on emptiness.

In brief, a practitioner of *lo-jong* should consider anyone who harms him to be a kind friend who brings an opportunity to practise the bodhimind. One only becomes aware of one's weaknesses and delusions when put to the test, so the harmer is actually an emanation of one's teacher or of the Buddhas. When we become ill we usually forget our samsaric, superficial plans and remember Dharma; thus the illness should be seen as a manifestation of the enlightened activity of the Buddhas. We can generate bodhimind by correctly relying upon harms and diseases just as surely as by relying upon a Guru, so these must be messengers of the Guru.

B. TRANSFORMING NEGATIVITIES THROUGH ACCUMULATION
AND PURIFICATION

Transforming negative conditions into the path by means of the activities of accumulating creative energy and purifying the mind of negative conditions is introduced by the following lines in the *Root Text :*

Having the four activities is the supreme method.

The four are: (1) accumulating spiritual energy and wisdom; (2) purifying evil; (3) making offerings to spirits; and (4) making offerings to the Dharma Protectors.

(1) When suffering arises and you wish to be free of it, you should think, "If I would rather have happiness than suffering, this suffering is a sign that I should collect the causes of happiness." Make offerings to the Three Jewels of Refuge, serve the

Sangha, make offerings to the Dharma Protectors and local spirits, etc., and strive with your body, speech and mind to amass spiritual energy. Take refuge in the Triple Gem and repeatedly recollect the bodhimind. Make devotions to your spiritual master and make the following request to him, "If it is best for me to become ill, grant me power to become ill. If it is best that I stay healthy, grant me powers of health. If it is best that I live long, grant me blessings for a long life. And if it is best that I die now, grant me blessings to die correctly." Such is the prayer that transcends worldy hopes.

(2) You should also think, "If I do not wish to have sufferings, then this suffering I now am experiencing is but a sign that I should purify myself of karmic and psychic negativity, the cause of suffering." With this view in mind, apply the four opponent forces in conjunction with laying bare all your faults and shortcomings.

(3) Whenever bothered by evil spirits, offer them ritual cakes (*Skt. balim*) and then request them, "O kind friends who assist us yogis in our efforts to develop the bodhimind; pray, cause the suffering of others to ripen upon me."

If you are unable to do this, then meditate upon love and compassion, offer them ritual cakes and then say to them, "May all my present activities benefit you both immediately and eternally. I request you, do nothing to obstruct my Dharma practices."

(4) Also, make offerings of ritual cakes to the Dharma Protectors, saying to them, "Pacify all conditions hindering my Dharma practice and bestow your magical actions which produce conducive conditions."

As for transforming unexpected events into the path to enlightenment, the *Root Text* states,

> *Meditate upon whatever occurs.*

Whenever illness, accidents, spirits or violent people come

into your life, recollect that many people in the world must
suffer from similar difficulties and meditate upon compassion.
Think, ''May I take all of their sufferings upon myself.''

IV. THE DOCTRINE OF A PRACTICE FOR ONE LIFETIME.

The *Root Text* states,
> *The essence of this teaching abbreviates*
> *Into the application of the five powers.''*

The five are: determination, familiarity, the white seed, accumulation and aspiration.

Determination: This is the thought to practise the two types
of bodhimind until enlightenment is attained, and never to become seperated from them. It should be generated again and
again.

Familarity: Meditate repeatedly upon the two types of bodhimind.

Accumulation: In order to give birth to what bodhimind has
not yet been born within you, as well as to increase that which
you have previously generated, strive to accumulate both goodness and wisdom.

The White Seed: Whenever self-cherishing arises, remember
that all the suffering experienced since beginningless time has
its source purely in self-cherishing. Even the suffering that one
presently experiences is a product of it. Continually maintain

the thought, "May I never act on the basis of self-cherishing, the deepest of enemies "

Aspiration: After completing any creative action, think, "In all future lives may I never become seperated from the two types of bodhimind. May I have strength to welcome anything that happens to me as a friend come to help me in the practice of the two bodhiminds."

How are these five powers to be applied at the time of death? The *Root Text* states,

The Mahayana precept of transmigration
Lies in these five powers.
And cherish the death posture.

The Power of the White Seed: When dying, give away all your possessions to spiritually valid causes and abide within non-attachment for sensual objects.

Aspiration: Make offerings to your spiritual teacher and to the Three Jewels, requesting them, "Bestow power upon me to always practise and never to become seperated from the two bodhiminds throughout the *bar-do* and in all future lives. Bestow power upon me to meet constantly with spiritual friends who will further guide me in the Dharma of the two bodhiminds." Repeat this again and again while dying.

Determination: Make firm the thought to practise the bodhi-mind throughout the *bar-do* and all future lives.

Familiarity: As you die, try to meditate deeply upon the two bodhiminds.

The words "cherish the death posture" means that when dying you should lie upon your right side with the palm of your right hand under the cheek of your face and the little finger of the right hand closing off the right nostril. All breath should pass solely through the left nostril. The mouth should be kept lightly closed.

Meditate upon love and compassion and pass away with the mind placed in the sphere of "giving and taking."

V. THE SIGNS OF PROGRESS

The *Root Text* states,

   All Dharmas condense into one theme.

All the various teachings of both the Hinayana and the Mahayana traditions have but one objective in mind: to tame ego-grasping. When the opponents to ego-grasping gain the upper hand, this is a sign that progress in *lo-jong* is being made.

The *Root Text* states,

   Hold to the chief of the two witnesses.

Other people who see and judge our practice are a type of witness; but more important than them is one's own mind, which can see and judge how much and with what strength the self-cherishing attitude arises. If we have little need to criticise ourselves, our practice has produced some results.

The *Root Text* states,

   The mind constantly relies upon joy alone.

By the strength of correct *lo-jong* practice, even the worst interference or negative condition can be turned into an aid on the path. He whose practice has progressed, transcends anxiety and worry over physical circumstances. He constantly abides in happiness and joy.

The *Root Text* states,
> *If there is ability*
> *Even when wandering,*
> *This is a sign of progress.*

An expert horseman is not thrown by an unexpected movement of his horse. Likewise, when a sudden problem occurs and we have no time to apply the opponents, yet we are still able to transform the event into an aid in the practice of spiritual transformation, progress has been made.

VI COMMITMENTS OF *LO-JONG* PRACTICE

The *Root Text* states,
> *Constantly train in the three general points.*

The three are: (A) not transgressing the commitments of practice; (B) not wasting yourself with ego games; and (C) not falling into partisanship.

(A) A true practitioner of the *lo-jong* tradition of spiritual transformation abandons the attitude of disregarding seemingly minor commitments of the system. You should guard yourself against degeneration of all commitments that you hold, whether of the Hinayana, Mahayana or Vajrayana.

(B) Avoid boasting and showing off any supposed attainments, such as by saying, "I have no self-cherishing, so I am above the harmful powers of others. Therefore in order to benefit others I can cut down trees in which malignant spirits dwell, or can live with people who have contagious diseases such as leprosy, etc." Practise in accordance with the examples set by the early Kadampa masters.

(C) Some *lo-jong* practitioners accept the harms done to them by humans, but when ghosts or spirits disturb them they re-

taliate with especially wrathful mantras. Others have respect
for people of high status but disdain for the lowly, or have
affection for friends and relatives but aversion for enemies.
Avoid such partisan tendencies if you would practise the *lo-jong*
tradition of spiritual transformation.

The *Root Text,*
> *Do not speak about weakened limbs.*

Avoid speaking about the faults of others, whether physical
faults such as handicaps or abnormalities, or faults of practice
such as the degeneration of vows.

The *Root Text,*
> *Do not judge others.*

Whenever you seem to perceive faults in other sentient beings
in general, or, more specifically, in other Dharma practitioners,
blame the imperfection upon your own impure perception.
Consider the fault to lie within yourself, not within them. Think
of everyone except yourself as being faultless.

The *Root Text,*
> *Purify the strongest delusion first.*

Continually analyse the condition of your mind and determine
exactly what is your worst hindrance. Concentrate upon purifying it immediately.

The *Root Text,*
> *Abandon all expectations.*

Avoid practising this tradition of spiritual transformation on
grounds such as hoping to gain fame or material benefits in this
life, or to gain a high rebirth such as a human or god, or even to
achieve the state of nirvana for yourself.

The *Root Text,*
> *Avoid food mixed with poison.*

Mixing poison with good food results in death. The food, intended to aid physical well-being, has the opposite effect. Similarly, mixing self-cherishing into our spiritual practices extinguishes the life of liberation and knowledge. Keep all practices free from self-cherishing.

The *Root Text*,
> *Do not be lenient toward the wrong object.*

Perhaps when others are good to us we feel affectionate toward them, but toward those who harm us we feel aversion. Or we feel kindness even toward those who harm us, but toward our own delusions we feel lenient. These attitudes contradict spiritual transformation.

The *Root Text*,
> *Do not mock weakness.*

If you see a weakness or abnormality in others, do not agitate it by mocking and teasing them about it.

The *Root Text*,
> *Do not strike sensitive areas.*

That is to say, if someone is hiding faults or secrets, do not involve yourself by revealing him publically. Or when gods or ghosts create disturbances, do not use the exceedingly wrathful mantras on them.

The *Root Text*,
> *Do not put the load of a dzo on a bullock.*

If unpleasant works are on the horizon, do not connive to direct them away from yourself and onto others.

The *Root Text*,
> *Do not hurry.*

If you should see some object or position you want that is of long-term benefit to you, do not sacrifice your integrity or accept temporary belittling from others as a means of gaining it.

The *Root Text*,
> *Do not turn a god into a devil.*

Although worldly gods are usually of benefit to those who worship them, occasionally when the devotees have improper attitudes toward them they become malicious and cause harm. Thus the god becomes a devil. Similarly, the purpose of spiritual practice is to purify delusion; but sometimes it happens that spiritual practice just increases a man's pride and arrogance. Thus a medicine is turned into a poison, and a god into a devil. Avoid this pitfall.

The *Root Text*,
> *Do not rejoice in sorrow.*

Do not take causes of other people's sorrow as conditions for your own happiness. For example, if a parent, relative or friend dies and as a result we inherit wealth, texts, statues or other material benefits, we should not rejoice in the event as being positive. Perhaps a sponsor dies and we receive gifts from his family; or a contemporary or a competitor dies and our position improves by his absence. Or an enemy dies and we think, "Ah good, now he can't harm me anymore." These are not exactly joyous occasions, and any benefit that comes from them should be viewed accordingly.

VII. GENERAL ADVICE FOR MAHAYANA *LO-JONG* PRACTITIONERS

The *Root Text*,
> *Practise all yogas in one manner.*

Use all activities, such as eating, putting on clothing, etc., as yogas aimed at benefitting others. Whatever you do, direct it solely to the benefit of others.

The *Root Text*,
> *Face all discouragements in one manner.*

Sometimes people who have just begun meditating upon the *lo-jong* tradition meet with an unusually large number of problems, such as sickness, ghosts, demons, angry people, delusions and so forth. These arise within the stream of their being with an even greater intensity than before they began practising, and they become greatly discouraged. At such moments, remember that in this world there are countless people experiencing similar difficulties. Develop a sense of compassion for them and practise the meditation "giving and taking" —taking their difficulties through the power of your own problems and giving them all goodness and joy.

The *Root Text*,
> *Engage two practices:*
> *One at the beginning and one at the end.*

As soon as you get out of bed in the morning, generate the thought, "Today may I not become seperated from awareness of the two types of bodhimind—the altruistic mind of enlightenment and the altruistic mind perceiving emptiness." Throughout the day remind yourself of this determination and before going to bed at night meditate upon your activities of the day. Analyse them to determine whether or not you have contradicted the bodhimind ideal. If you did contradict it, discipline yourself and apply the four remedies in order to purify yourself of the transgression. If you didn't contradict it, meditate upon joy and determine to practise equally well in the future.

The *Root Text*,
> *Maintain patience for both.*

Whenever you receive material benefits, praises or any kind of success, do not be proud or pleased. Consider it as an illusion and use it solely as a means to benefit others. Alternatively, when-

ever you lose material standing, are scorned, fail in your efforts
and become so down that only water can get under you, do not
become discouraged. Rather, consider how in this world many
people are down and meditate upon "giving and taking": taking
all their poverty and failures upon yourself through the power
of your own failure, and giving them all goodness and joy.

The *Root Text*,
  Guard two things like you would your life.
Protect both the general commitments of altruism and the
altruistic commitments of this tradition of spiritual transformation as you would guard your very life.

The *Root Text*,
  Train in the three difficult practices.
These three are: the difficult practice of checking a delusion
with its specific remedy as soon as the delusion arises; the difficult practice of successfully reversing the delusion; and the difficult practice of eventually severing the delusion from your mindstream entirely. Train in these three by being quick to attack
any delusion that arises within you, by persisting until the delusion is reversed, and by persisting relentlessly until the delusion
is utterly severed.

The *Root Text*,
  Cultivate the three principal causes.

Of the many causes of religious practices, the three principal
causes are: meeting with a spiritual friend who can inspire and
teach us; developing the ability to digest the teachings and to
apply them to our own stream of being; and having the spiritual
stability necessary in order to maintain all the conditions suitable
to religious practice. If you have all three of these qualities,
rejoice in your good fortune and make the wish that all other

sentient beings may come to possess them as well. If you don't
have all of them, consider how in this world there are many who,
like you, do not possess all three principal causes of religious
practice. Meditate on taking their shortcomings upon yourself
and offer the hope that they all might come to possess all three
causes.

The *Root Text,*
   Meditate on the three unmitigated qualities.

The most important of all the Mahayana practices is to meditate with admiration and confidence upon the spiritual teacher.
Meditate thus with unmitigated strength.

The quintessence of all Mahayana practices is this tradition
of spiritual transformation. Meditate on it with unmitigated joy.

Lastly, have unmitigated zeal in maintaining even the very
subtle trainings.

The *Root Text,*
   Possess the three inseparables.

With your body, continually prostrate to the objects of refuge,
circumambulate the temples and reliquaries, and so forth. With
your speech, continually recite the profound scriptures, prayers,
dharanis, mantras and so forth. And with your mind, meditate
continually upon love, compassion and the two types of bodhimind. Never seperate your body, speech and mind from these
three practices.

The *Root Text,*
   Practise without bias toward the objects.

Do not discriminate between ordinary and holy beings in your
practice. One cannot tell who is really holy and who is not, so
treat all equally well.

The *Root Text,*
   Embrace everything and cherish all from the heart.

Whatever arises in your mind, embrace it with the teachings on spiritual transformation. Cherish all sentient beings not in mere words, but within the deepest recesses of your heart.

The *Root Text*,

> *Constantly practise on special cases.*

Whenever we encounter competitors, enemies, someone who has harmed us without reason, or someone toward whom, even though he hasn't harmed us, we feel a strong aversion because of karma from previous lives, we should consider these to be special envoys sent to help us in our practice of spiritual transformation. Constantly regard them with extra care.

The *Root Text*,

> *Do not rely upon external conditions.*

Generally, common people like to have conditions conducive to religious practice and to avoid difficult conditions such as harms from men or ghosts. But in the *lo-jong* tradition we just take whatever comes —inharmonious conditions or difficulties— and transform them into aids on the spiritual path.

The *Root Text*,

> *Immediately accomplish what is important.*

The countless previous lives we have taken throughout beginningless time have largely been in vain, for we are not yet enlightened. But at the moment we have a human form able to attain ultimate perfection and we should immediately use it to accomplish that which is important.

What is important? It is more important to benefit the mind than to benefit the body. The practice of religion, which benefits here and hereafter, is much more important than worldly works, which benefit this life alone. As for religion, it is more important to know a little and to practise it well than to know much but to practise it poorly. Within the various practices, meditation upon the two types of bodhimind is most important. Also, more important than gaining an understanding based upon scriptures or upon one's limited reasoning is to rely upon the oral teachings of a spiritual master and to meditate perfectly in accord with his instructions. In terms of activities, the most important is meditation. And lastly, more important than physically renouncing the infinite objects of attachment is to develop a renounced mind. These are the important subjects to be mastered.

The *Root Text*,
    Avoid wrong understanding.

That is to say, do not practise the six wrong attitudes:—

(i) Wrong enthusiasm: not having true zest for Dharma but having it for the pleasures and possessions of this life.

(ii) Wrong patience: not having patience for difficult religious practices, but having it for worldly activities such as competing with enemies and helping friends.

(iii) Wrong taste: having no taste for religious activities such as listening to teachings, contemplating or meditating, but having a taste for the pleasures of transient existence alone.

(iv) Wrong compassion: not meditating on compassion for people who live in luxury gained through evil deeds, but feeling it for ascetics and yogis who, in order to practise religion, undergo hardships and difficulties.

(v) Wrong encouragement: encouraging those who rely upon us to seek material security and social improvement rather than encouraging them to seek the eternal benefit of spiritual realisation.

(vi) Wrong rejoicing: rather than rejoicing in goodness and spritual joys of a transcendental nature, rejoicing in worldly success and material achievements.

The *Root Text,*
> *Do not practise with irregularity.*

Do not be unstable in your practice of *lo-jong*, today meditating intensely and tomorrow doing nothing at all. Maintain a continuous, steady effort in practice.

The *Root Text,*
> *Practise with confidence.*

The divided mind is a weak mind; do not rely upon it. Have complete confidence in your abilities and apply yourself to the practices from the very recesses of your heart.

The *Root Text,*
> *Think deeply with insight and analysis.*

That is to say, carefully observe your stream of actions, words and thoughts and determine what are the effects of delusion and what the effects of wisdom. Then meditate and apply the opponent forces to all manifest delusion. This is applied insight. Then check again and see whether the delusion has been abandoned or not. If it has not, regenerate the opponent forces and eliminate it.

The *Root Text,*
> *Do not become familiar with vanity.*

If you benefit someone or complete some type of difficult religious practice, do not entertain pride. The theme of the *lo-jong* tradition is to meditate upon cherishing others. There is no place in it for conceit or vanity.

The *Root Text,*
> *Do not respond with arrogance.*

If someone criticises you at a gathering of people, do not speak back in defence of yourself. Turn the criticism and your responses to it into a direct remedy to grasping at a self-nature in the objects of existence.

The *Root Text*,
> *Do not be inconsistent.*

A person who at the slightest provocation changes from a harmonious to an upset mind makes life difficult indeed for those around him and hinders his own and others' religious practice. Be consistent in your dealings with others.

The *Root Text*,
> *Have no expectations.*

Whenever you do something to benefit someone else or make great exertions in a particular meditation or spiritual exercise, do not expect visible results. Practise purely for the sake of practice. The results will take care of themselves.

The Colophon: Notes on an oral discourse given by Gyalwa Gendun Drub to an open audience.

BIBLIOGRAPHY OF TEXTS QUOTED

Friendly Letter
Tib. *bShes-'prin* (T.)

Twenty Pledges
Tib. *SDom-pa-nyi-bcu* (T.)

A Guide to the Bodhisattva's Way of Life
Tib. *Byang-chub-sems-dpai-spyod-pa-la-'jug-pa* (T.)

Chapter Three:

Two Texts on Emptiness

Text One: Turning Toward Emptiness

Through contemplating the general shortcomings of samsara and also the specific miseries of the individual realms of the world, an understanding of the unsatisfactory nature of un-enlightened existence arises. At that moment the mind which seeks liberation from samsaric suffering is experienced for the first time.

What is the source of samsaric misery? Virtuous and non-virtuous actions tainted by contaminated perception. What is the source of these actions? The three psychic poisons: attachment, aversion and ignorance. Finally, ignorance is the deepest of these three, for from ignorance do attachment and aversion arise. Moreover, since the very heart of ignorance is the innate grasping at an "I", anyone who wishes to attain full liberation from all forms of suffering must strive to abandon this subtle, inborn ego-grasping.

To abandon ego-grasping one must discern and meditate on emptiness, or non-inherent existence. The method for doing so is as follows.

Begin by examining this ostensibly self-existent I. Were it to have true existence, then it would have to do so either upon one or more of the five psychophysical aggregates of being (i.e., form, feeling, perception, volitional archetypes and primary consciousness), upon all five as a composite group, or else somewhere removed from these five.

As for the first of these three possibilities, none of the aggregates are the inherently existent I; for if we refer this I to any of the five aggregates, asking ourselves, "Is this aggregate merely 'my aggregate' or is it the 'I'; or is the 'I' the aggregate," very spontaneously we get an answer that the aggregate is not the I, and the I is not the aggregate. This occurs equally clearly with with all five aggregates.

It is equally impossible for this I to exist on the five aggregates as a whole. Buddha himself said:

Just as the label chariot is given
In dependence upon a collection of parts,
Similarly in reliance upon the five aggregates
We conventionally have sentient beings.

Also Chandrakirti states in his *A Guide to the Middle View:*

The sutras say that in reliance upon
The five aggregates does "I" arise.
Thus the I is not the aggregates themselves.

Moreover, the I could not exist anywhere outside the aggregates. If it could, then when we take away the five aggregates we would be left with the innately produced I. However, nothing outside the five aggregates could possibly function as a receptacle for this I. This is quickly revealed through meditative analysis.

Thus, as the innately produced I is not any of the individual aggregates, is not the collection of them nor does it exist anywhere apart from them, it would seem that it does not exist at all. This is how we should meditate.

During meditation sessions we should try to generate an awareness of the non-existence of the innate conception of "I". Between sessions we should continually remember that, although the I conventionally appears to be self-existent, in fact it is non-existent and is like a thing seen in a dream, like a magician's creation.

In addition, during the post-meditation periods one should contemplate how all the numberless sentient beings, grasping at this innately existent I, experience the infinite forms of samsaric suffering; yet there is not one of them who has not been our friend and relative in countless past lives. Again and again they have been my mother, providing me with all the kindness and benefits that a mother performs and protecting me from harm. We should think, "May they all become free from suffering and its cause: this very grasping at an inherently existent self. I myself will free them from suffering and its cause. In order to be able to effectively accomplish this, may I attain sublime and peerless enlightenment."

This is how to generate insight into the selflessness of persons (i.e., of sentient beings) during both meditation and post-meditation periods.

As for meditation upon the selflessness of phenomena, during sittings meditate how the various phenomena are non-inherently existent, following a line of observation similar to that described above. If something exists in an object to inherently represent it, does it do so within any of the individual parts, within the arrangement of the parts or in a place separate from these two? Between sittings, contemplate how the events that are perceived,

such as seeds and sprouts, are not truly existent. A sprout has
no inherent nature, for it is born from causes and sustained by
conditions. By continually directing one's thoughts like this,
everything that appears becomes seen in the light of emptiness
and the conventional reality of causality arises as evidence of
emptiness. On the other hand, by contemplating how all dharmas are non-inherently existent yet as non-inherently existent
dharmas continue to function on the conventional plane, emptiness arises as the meaning of causality.

Through gaining familiarity with the teachings on emptiness
by training in both meditation sittings and post-meditational
contemplation, one generates a state of meditative quiesence
(*Skt. samatha*) focussed upon emptiness. This brings one to
the 'path of collection', first of the five paths to enlightenment.
Persistence in insight meditation (*Skt, vipassyana*) upon emptiness brings one to the second of the five paths, the 'path of
application'. Next one gains direct meditative experience of
emptiness, which places one on the third path, the 'path of
direct vision'. Prolonged meditation absorbed in a direct vision
of emptiness gradually transports one across the fourth path,
the 'path of meditation'. Finally, by persisting in the practices
of the path of meditation one gradually abandons the I-grasp-
ing ignorance together with the infinite variety of delusions and
sufferings that are born from it, thus attaining liberation and
entering the 'path beyond practice', the Great Union Beyond
Practice, which is the inseparability of the innately born great
bliss that understands emptiness with the Beatific Body born
from infinite goodness. This is the ultimate attainment, the
state of final illumination.

Yet in order to accomplish the Great Union Beyond Practice,
the Great Union of Practice must first be accomplished: for
the Great Union Beyond Practice requires a cause sharing its
own nature. Moreover, to accomplish the Great Union
of Practice one must first accomplish the fourth stage—that

of clear light—for from the subtle mind of clear light and the subtle energies which act as the vehicle of this mind is the body of the Great Union of Practice produced. Therefore, as a preliminary to the fourth stage, or clear light realization, one must generate the third stage, that of the astral or illusory body; for the fourth stage, or clear light realization, arises from the purification experienced by entering into the clear light by means of generating and controlling the astral or illusory body.

A prerequisite to the third stage, or realization of the illusory body, is the yoga of mind isolation; for the vital energies and states of consciousness that arise from the yoga of mind isolation are instrumental in giving birth to the illusory body. Moreover, mind isolation must be preceded by mastery of the vajra breathing techniques; for it is only by the strength of meditating upon the mystic drops and the energies that course through the three channels that the most subtle energies are encouraged to enter the heart, an indispensible condition to the accomplishment of mind isolation. Finally, vajra breathing must be preceded by the yoga of body isolation; for previous to the stages of withdrawing subtle energies to the heart one must gain control over the mystic drops and the coarser energies and must concentrate these on the mystic pressure points, meditating on bliss and emptiness while coursing on subtle energies held in the central channel.

Between sessions one must engage creative imagination to experience all that appears within the sphere of great bliss, and to see that it is this very bliss that arises in the form of the deities of the blissful mandala.

To practise the above tantric yogas of Great Union, clear light, the illusory body, mind isolation, vajra breathing and body isolation, one must first accomplish subtle insight that renders the mind mature; and before this one must accomplish the yoga of coarse single-pointed mindfulness. Moreover, throughout one's practice one should closely protect the vows and

commitments that were taken at the time of initiation. Both
the initiation, and its instruction should be received from a
qualified teacher. As a preliminary to initiation the disciple
must generate the bodhimind through a technique such as the
'six causes and one effect'—recognising that all sentient beings
have once been one's mother, generating awareness of the
kindness of a mother, the wish to repay the kindness of the
infinite sentient beings, the beautiful mind of love that wants
happiness for all, compassion that wishes to see all beings free
of suffering, the extraordinary attitude of universal responsibility; and the effect, the supreme bodhimind that seeks enlightenment in order to be able to serve the world most
effectively. As a preliminary to meditation upon the bodhimind
one should meditate upon the general and specific miseries
of samsaric existence and thus give birth to the mind that yearns
for liberation; and to support the practices bringing liberation
one should abandon all forms of evil, the cause of misery, and
cultivate every goodness, the cause of happiness. Also, as a
preliminary to these disciplines of cause and effect one should
practise sustained mindfulness of death. Finally, as a preliminary to meditation upon death one should meditate upon the
freedoms and endowments afforded by human existence and
on the difficulty of finding such an auspicious opportunity again
in the future if nothing is accomplished with this life.

BIBLIOGRAPHY OF TEXTS QUOTE.

A Guide to the Middle View.

Tib. dBu-ma-'jug-pa (T.)

Text Two : A Rosary of Gems

A Commentary to the meaning of Nagarjuna's *Fundamental Treatise on the Wisdom of Emptiness*, Chapter XXIV.

The master (Nagarjuna) opens (the chapter "An Analysis of Truth") with a presentation of the arguments thrown against him by those who diasgree with his view that nothing —including the four noble truths—has true existence. He follows this with his reply to their qualms.

THE ARGUMENTS OF HIS OPPONENTS

It follows that you negate the existence of the creation and dissolution (of impermanent phenomena) as well as the four noble truths themselves; for you say that these are all empty (of true existence).

Therefore there is no knowledge (of the truth of suffering), no abandonment (of the true causes of suffering), no meditation (upon the true path leading to the cessation of suffering), and no attainment (of the state of true cessation); for the four noble truths are themselves without true existence.

This means that there are no four goals (i.e., stream enterer, once returner, never returner and Arhant); for knowledge (of suffering), abandonment (of its cause), meditation (on the path) and attainment (of a state of cessation of suffering) do not exist.

As the four goals are non-existent, there are neither the four abiders in the goals nor the four enterers into the goals. This means that there is also no Sangha; for the above eight types of spiritual beings (that constitute the Sangha) do not exist.

Also there is no Dharma; for the (four) noble truths (on which the validity of Dharma depends) do not exist.

How then can there be Buddha?—for Dharma and the Sangha are non-existents.

Thus the very existence of the Three Jewels becomes destroyed when you proclaim the doctrine that all things are without self-nature and thus abide in emptiness.

An accomplished philosopher, an irreligious person, the Dharma itself and even the views of ordinary, common people: all of their existence has been destroyed; for (you say that) all things are by self-nature empty of inherent being.

NAGARJUNA'S REPLY

The Master's reply to these arguments has four parts: (A) showing that causality (dependent origination) has been misunderstood; (B) showing emptiness as the very point of causality (i.e., the relative level of truth); (C) showing the shortcomings of tenets contradicting the theory of emptiness; and (D) showing that if the Thatness of causality is seen, the ultimate nature of the four noble truths also is seen.

(A) The passage demonstrating that causality has been misunderstood has two outlines: (1) the actual presentation; and (2) comparing the validity of his own and other's views.

(1) The actual presentation has two parts: (a) showing that their arguments suffer from three misunderstandings; and (b) showing that his opponents have not understood the two levels of truth.

(a) The exponents of inherent existence interpret the words "empty of true existence" to mean total non-existence, which contradicts their doctrines; for they do not understand the purpose for which the doctrine of emptiness was expounded; the nature of emptiness, nor the essential meaning of emptiness.

The doctrine of emptiness was expounded in order to eliminate grasping at true existence. Its nature is the pacification of distorted perception. And its essential meaning is simply "empty of inherent existence."

(b) Their misunderstanding of the two levels of truth is dealt with in five sections: (i) the nature of the two truths; (i) showing that if one does not understand the two levels of truth one will miscomprehend the essential meaning of all the scriptures; (iii) the purpose for which the doctrine of the two levels of truth was expounded; (iv) the shortcomings of holding incorrect views concerning the nature of the two levels of truth; and (v) explaining that because it is difficult to correctly comprehend the doctrine of the two levels of truth, it should not be taught to beginners.

(i) While not understanding the purpose, nature or meaning of emptiness, they seek to criticise the doctrine of emptiness.

Who are they? The very people who do not correctly differentiate the two levels of truth! However, one must have correctly understood these two levels in order to have reversed incorrect understanding. Thus these are the very people for whom the doctrine of the two truths was expounded.

The Dharma taught by the Buddhas rests upon the doctrine

of the two levels of truth; for it is composed of doctrines dealing with the illusory, conventional level of truth and of docto-
rines dealing with the truth of ultimate significance.

(ii) The exponents of inherent existence do not fully comprehend the profound Thatness of the Buddhadharma; for
they do not understand how to differentiate correctly between
the two truths.

(iii) The doctrine of the two truths has a purpose: if the
conventional truth is not relied upon, one does not become
a vessel to whom the ultimate truth can be revealed; and until
the ultimate level has been perceived, nirvana cannot be attained.

(iv) Those who expound true existence, being of limited wisdom, fall down when they learn of emptiness; for their understanding remains faulty. They are like the man who grabs a snake
incorrectly; or like the sorcerer who mispronounces his magical
spells.

(v) The (emptiness of) objects of knowledge, being a dharma
difficult for those of feeble mind to fathom, was said by the
Awakened One to lead only to downfall when taught to the
unprepared; for the shortcomings of apprehending emptiness
incorrectly indeed are great.

(2) O exponents of inherent existence, the various faults you
see in the doctrine of emptiness are invalid to me, who holds
the Middle View; for you speak of the annihilation of creation,
dissolution, the four noble truths and so on; but to an exponent
of emptiness this is not considered (to be self-evident).

The Middle View is the valid tenet; for wherever one looks
one finds this view of emptiness to be sound. On the other hand,
the exponents of inherent existence hold distorted tenets; for
their views on emptiness miss the point.

O exponents of inherent existence, you try to turn the faults
of your doctrine into faults of the Middle View. You simply

take whatever arises and try to call it a fault in the doctrine of emptiness. You are like the man on a horse who forgets that in fact he is riding.

You who expound inherent existence: It follows that you must think that things have neither causes nor conditions; for if you say that things have inherent existence, then the view arising from it leads to that conclusion. For the same reason you are also negating the functioning of cause, effect, a doer, the act of doing, the deed itself, creation, dissolution, and attainment.

(b) As for the objects of knowledge, they are not something not having emptiness as their ultimate nature; for anything that is not a dependent arising is not an existent. This is so because it is said that wherever there is a dependent arising there is emptiness; and wherever there is emptiness there is a dependent arising. Such are the philosophical attitudes of those holding to the Middle View free from extremes.

(C) Nagarjuna's presentation of the shortcomings of tenets contradicting the doctrine of emptiness has three sections: (1) showing how they destroy the four noble truths as well as knowledge of them, etc.; (2) how they destroy the validity of the Three Jewels, spiritual learning, practice, etc.; and (3) how they are in discord with the views of worldly and non-worldy people alike.

(1) As for the exponents of inherent existence, if follows that they are negating evolution, dissolution, and so forth; for they say that none of these phenomena abide in emptiness. Consequently it follows that they are also negating the four noble truths; for if there is no evolution and so forth, how can suffering and the other noble truths come into existence? The very teachings on impermanence and suffering themselves have no true existence.

If suffering were not empty of inherent existence, it could not have a true source; for were its nature to have an inherent status, it would not be able to change or evolve. Also, the state of the cessation of suffering could not exist; for you say that the existence of suffering is inherent. As that which is inherently existent cannot change, how can inherently existent suffering ever be destroyed? Its nature must be constant. Therefore by denying the doctrine of emptiness you are denying the teaching on the noble truth of the cessation of suffering.

Similarly, meditation upon the true path leading to cessation of suffering would be of no avail; for one's experience of the path, having inherent existence, could not evolve. Therefore, (my view is that) the path cannot be an inherently existent phenomena; for it is an object cultivated by meditation.

(You say that if I believe that things are empty of having true existence) then it is not correct to think that by meditating on the path one will attain the cessation of suffering; for suffering, its source and its cessation are all non-existent. However, (for he who advocates the inherent existence) of suffering, it follows that (if he does not now have) complete knowledge of suffering, he will never be able to gain it; for the previous non-existence of this knowledge had an inherent status. To be inherent, it must either inherently exist or inherently not exist.

Thus (by abandoning the doctrine of emptiness) you are saying that (the teachings on) the truth of suffering, the truth of its cause, the state of cessation, meditation upon the path leading to cessation, and also the four spiritual goals are invalid; for any sources of suffering that have not yet been abandoned will have inherent existence. The problem is the same as with an inherently existent limited knowledge of suffering.

As for the four spiritual goals, how could an ordinary person gain the ability to attain them in the future? It would be impossible; for (you say that) the previous non-attainment had inherent existence. If it has an inherent nature, there will be no way to reverse the inherency.

(2) Moreover, (by abandoning the doctrine of emptiness you are saying that) there are no attainers of the four goals, nor enterers into the goals; for the goals are thus rendered unattainable (one's previous non-attainment having been inherently existent). Therefore there is no Sangha, for the eight types of spiritual beings cannot exist. The Dharma also must be non-existent; for the four noble truths upon which it relies have been negated. How, then, can there be a Buddha? There could not be; for the Dharma (that he would have had to practise in order to gain Buddhahood) and the Sangha (who would aid him in attaining his goal) have been destroyed. Therefore, your Buddha cannot depend upon enlightenment and your enlightenment cannot depend upon a Buddha; for that Buddha and that enlightenment are both inherently existent.

(In your system) there is no hope that an ordinary being who engages in the Bodhisattva practices in order to attain Buddhahood will attain his goal; for the state of non-Buddhahood (in which he presently finds himself) is inherently existent.

A person would be unable to do either virtuous or evil actions; for how can that which is not empty of an intrinsic nature engage in activity? Action implies change. In inherent existence there can be no action.

Even though you did not do either a virtuous or an evil action, the karmic results of having done so would come to you; and although you were to create a virtuous or an evil action, the karmic fruits would not come to you; for the fruits would have inherent existence (and therefore would not need to depend upon a specific karmic cause).

How can karmic fruits that ripen from specific causes such as a virtuous or an evil acton not be empty of having an inherent nature? They are empty of inherence, for they are entities produced in dependence upon causes.

(3) The exponent of true existence is also in discord with the conventional views of worldly people; for he denies the

emptiness of causality. By so doing he is saying that a specific action will produce no fruit, that without effort the fruits of actions will arise, and that there would be a doer (of an action) without him having to depend upon the action of doing. The living beings would be without birth and without death. They would be of a static, non-evolving nature. The events in their lives would occur at random, (i.e., without any relation to their own actions); for their existence, being inherent, would not have to depend upon causes or conditions. The unattained could not be attained and the levels of suffering as well as karma and delusion could not be abandoned; for (you say that) they are not empty of having an intrinsic nature.

(D) As for objects of knowledge, the person who sees them as being interdependent phenomena empty of having true existence will also see the ultimate nature of suffering, its source, the cessation of suffering and the path leading to cessation; for he will realise that the beliefs of those expounding inherent existence are without a basis.

The Colophon: Thus ends "An Analysis of Truth," being a commentary to the essential meaning of Nagarjuna's "Mula-madhyamaka-karika-shastra, or" "Fundamental Treatise on Wisdom," Chapter XXIV.

Chapter IV:

Song of the Eastern Snow Mountains

Above the peaks of the eastern
snow mountains,
white clouds float high
in the sky.
There comes to me a vision
to my teacher.
Again and again am I reminded
of his kindness,
again and again am I moved
by faith.

To the east of the drifting
white clouds
lies the illustrious Ganden Monastery,
Hermitage of Joy.
There dwells three precious ones
difficult to describe—
my spiritual father Losang Trapa,
and his two chief sons.

Vast are your teaching on the
profound Dharma,
on the yogas of the path's
two stages.
To fortunate practitioners in this
land of snow mountains,
your kindness, O masters,
transcends thought.

That I, Gendun Drub, who tends
to be lazy,
now have a mind somewhat
propelled by Dharma,
is due solely to the great kindness
of this holy teacher and his
two chief disciples.
O perfect masters, your compassion
is indeed unsurpassed.

O three incomparable spiritual teachers,
from now until the essence
of illumination
I need seek no other refuge.
Pull me to enlightenment's shores
on the hooks of your mercy.

Although your kindness can never
be repaid,
O masters, still I pray to preserve
your lineages
at all times and with all
my strength,
never letting my thoughts fall prey
to either attachment or aversion.

These days in these remote
snow mountains
there are many men who would uphold
their own lineages
while looking down upon other
doctrine holders
verily as their deepest enemies.
Watching how they think and act,
my heart fills with sadness.

They boast that the lineage
they are following
is a high and superior path,
yet their motives are only to harm
other traditions
and their minds are chained
in hopes of fame.
If we analyse them closely,
are they not mere causes
of shame?

Finding themselves in their
old age
lost on barren paths far
from truth,
their spirits rage with
bitter jealousy
toward those who purely practise
true Dharma.
Have not demons
entered into their hearts?

For them to feel guilt over evils done
yet not to apply
the methods which counteract their causes,
the enemy Delusion,
is of as little value as placing
a demon trap at the
western door,
when in fact the demon
resides near the eastern door.

The true spiritual masters, who
understand this point,
look upon the living beings through
thoughts of love
and regard other teachers
with a deserved respect.
They seek to harm only the
enemy within themselves,
the enemy Delusion,

O friends who would follow
my tradition,
do not permit your minds
to wander aimlessly.
Constantly be mindful of your thoughts
and try by every means to remain
on the direct path to enlightenment.

Should any living beings ever heed
this small advice,
may they gain the compassionate bodhimind
and the view which understands the
ultimately pure sphere,
thus quickly attaining to the sublime glory
of supreme, peerless enlightenment.

May there rain forth auspicious signs
of the glorious spiritual masters,
their bodies ablaze with the marks of perfection,
their speech richly adorned with
the sixty qualities
and their minds a treasure of
profound knowledge and vast compassion.

Chapter V :

To Entice the Minds of the Wise

Notes on the two stages of yogic application in the Kalachakra Tantra

Homage to the feet of the Lama
Inseparably one with primordial Kalachakra.

A GENERAL PRESENTATION OF THE PATH

One should firstly train the mind by means of the ordinary Sutrayana methods. In specific, cultivate a definite understanding of the pure view of emptiness. Only then does one become spiritually ripe for receiving the initiations that permit one to enter the extraordinary Vajrayana path. Thereafter one should protect the vows and commitments made at the time of initiation as intensly as one protects one's life.

With this discipline as the basis, one can engage in the coarse and subtle yogas of the generation stage, which mature one's stream of being for practice of the completion stage. Finally, when these generation stage yogas have been taken to fulfillment one can enter into meditation upon the completion stage practices, together with their branches.

The result is the attainment of complete Buddhahood in the form of Kalachakra and Consort.

(*Commentary:* When Gendun Drub refers to Sutrayana practices, he means the methods for generating a mindstream tamed by an inner experience of the free spirit of renunciation and the Mahayana attitude of great compassion. The first of these is necessary in order to use lust as the path, a qualification of Highest Yoga Tantra; and the second is necessary in order to sublimate our experience of the wrathful symbols meditated upon.

In addition, if we do not approach the Vajrayana on the basis of a definite understanding of emptiness, our practice will be no better than that of the Hindu tantrikas and, rather than resulting in the full effect of Buddhahood, will produce only higher rebirth as a samsaric god.

Why is it necessary to receive initiation in order to practise the tantras? Just as someone who wishes to undertake a major building project must first obtain permission from the government, the spiritual aspirant wishing to undertake the great task of Vajrayana yoga must first gain the permission of a qualified lineage master. Moreover, at the time of initiation the master plants the seeds of tantric attainment within the mind of the disciple, and without these seeds our practice of the two tantric stages will be unable to produce the tree, branches and fruit of enlightenment.)

A DETAILED EXPLANATION

This will be presented under two headings: the initiations which make one into a proper vessel for tantric practice; and, having become a proper vessel, the path upon which one is to meditate.

The first of these involves four subjects: the mandala into which initiation is given; the number and stages of initiation; the nature of the individual initiations; and the purpose of initiation.

THE MANDALA INTO WHICH INITIATION IS GIVEN

The Mahasiddha Tilbupa writes, "There are three types of mandalas: those made from coloured chalk, those painted on canvas and those visualised in the body."

The *Tantra of the Secret Assembly* and also (Acharya Abhayakaragupta's) *Vajra Rosary of Initiation Rites* mentions the mandala of *dhyana,* or meditative absorption, as a fourth alternative.

(This, however, is speaking in general). The tradition of the *Kalachakra Tantra* is given in the *Treatise on the Initiations,* "There are seven initiations. The mandala should be constructed and these should be given. The basis is a mandala made from coloured chalk."

As clearly stated, and also as pointed out by Naropa in his *Commentary to the Treatise on the Initiations,* the Kalachakra initiations are only to be given into a mandala made of coloured chalk powder. Moreover, it is sufficient if the master performs solely the generation of the mind mandala. There is no need for him to invoke the deities of all three Kalachakra mandalas.

(*Commentary:* In tantras such as the *Heruka Chakrasambhara Tantra* and also the *Guhyasamaja Tantra*, any of the above four mandalas may be used as a basis of initiation. In Kalachakra, however, only a two dimentional mandala made from coloured chalk is used.

As in the *Chakrasambhara Tantra*, the Kalachakra system incorporates three mandalas—those of vajra body, speech and mind. In Kalachakra it is only necessary for the master to generate the latter of these as a preliminary to the initiation ceremony.)

THE NUMBER AND STAGES OF INITIATION

Generally it is said that there are eleven initiations: the seven of entering like a child, together with the four standard Highest Tantra initiations—vase, secret, wisdom and fourth. These latter four are given twice, the two phases being called the 'higher' and the 'higher-than-higher' initiations. However, as the names and nature of these are the same in both phases, they are grouped together. That is, both vase initiations are counted as one, and both secret as one. Both wisdom initiations, together with the fourth initiation of the first set, are also counted as one, as they all share the same nature. Finally, the fourth initiation of the higher-than-higher phase is counted by itself as the fourth initiation as it alone reveals the full meaning of enlightenment.

(*Commentary:* Most systems of Highest Tantra contain only four actual initiations—vase, secret, wisdom and word. In the Kalachakra system, the fourth of these is known simply as the fourth initiation. All four are given twice. This is unlike other Highest Tantras, where the four are given only once. Consequently it usually takes three rather than two days to give the full Kalachakra initiation.)

These two phases are preceded by the seven initiations of entering the mandala like a child enters the world. This process of spiritual rebirth is likened to the birth and stages in the growth of a child, such as washing, piercing the ears, giving earrings, encouraging the child to laugh and smile, etc. Thus are their names derived.

The initiation ceremony begins with the usual preliminaries (of taking refuge, generating the bodhimind), analysing the disciple, and so forth. One is then brought to the mandala and given the seven initiations of a child. These are followed by the four higher and then the four higher-than-higher initiations.

During the initiation one takes the pledge of secrecy and thereafter if one tells the secrets of Vajrayana to the uninitiated or to the spiritually immature, one's mystic link (*Skt. samaya*) with the tantra is broken. Similarly, if the Guru confuses the stages of initiation he creates the root downfall of speaking the higher secrets to the uninitiated; for the ceremony will be invalid and consequently even though the disciple hears the procedures he remains without initiation.

(*Commentary:* It is important that the initiating master here follows the correct stages of procedure. Otherwise, when he gives the higher initiations he is doing so to someone who has not received the lower and thus commits the error of speaking higher secrets to someone not holding the correct *samaya*.)

THE NATURE OF THE INITIATIONS

The seven initiations of entering like a child are each followed by the sprinkling of vase waters. Therefore they are also called the water initiations. The four faces of Kalachakra, which represent vajra body, speech, mind and wisdom, reveal the nature of these initiations.

First the disciple is shown the white face of vajra body which is in the north. This causes him to generate the vajra body. The four consorts residing in the mandala that has been produced bestow the water initiation and the five Tathagatas bestow the initiation of the vajra crown.

Next he is shown the red face of vajra speech, which is in the south. This causes him to generate vajra speech. The Ten Powerful Goddesses then bestow the initiation of the silk headress, and Kalachakra and Consort bestow the initiation of vajra and bell.

The disciple is now shown the black face of vajra mind, which is in the east. This causes him to generate the vajra mind. The heroes and heroines of the mandala then give the initiation of experience, and the male and female Wrathful Ones give the initiation of the word.

Finally the disciple is shown the yellow face of wisdom, which is in the west. This causes the vajra wisdom to be generated within him. Vajrasattva and Consort give him the initiation of permissions.

Anyone who attains these seven initiations and takes the practice of the generation stage to fulfillment shall become a master of the seven stages in this very life. Even if one is not able to complete these generation stage yogas before death strikes, this attainment will definately be achieved within seven lifetimes.

The main purpose of these seven initiations is to transform the spiritual aspirant into a vessel suitable for practice of the generation stage yogas and to provide a path for the cultivation of meditative stability. However, the initiations of the silk headress and of the vajra and bell also have the function of transforming the disciple into a vessel capable of the completion stage yogas, which gain control over the energies flowing through the secondary channels of the body and redirect them into *dhuti*, the central channel.

The next set of initiations, namely, the four higher initiations, have both generation and completion stage associations. For example, the nature of the vase initiation is as follows. The disciple is given a *mudra* possessing the appropriate characteristics. He holds her hand, strokes her breasts and so forth. The great bliss that arises introduces him to the vase initiation. Thus it is associated with the initiation of a master and is explained as the yoga of transforming lust into the path.

In this context the *Great Commentary* states, "The master accepts purified lust."

The secret initiation, second of the four higher initiations, is much the same as in other Highest Tantras, with the exception that when the blindfold is removed from the disciple's eyes he is told to look at the spreading vagina of a knowledge lady. Fierce passion arises within him, which in turn induces great bliss. This introduces him to the nature of the secret initiation.

The initiation of pristine wisdom is also much the same as in other tantras, although it is grouped together with the fourth initiation. The reason for this is that here the fourth initiation is so in name only. It does not possess the full characteristics of a fourth initiation and in fact shares the nature of the wisdom initiation. (This is evident from the symbolism meditated upon, which is as follows.) The disciple is given a knowledge lady and sits in union with her. The sexual substances come to the tip of his jewel, and the bliss thus induced introduces him to this fourth initiation. (As this bliss is in the nature of the wisdom initiation,) this fourth initiation is called 'the worldly fourth initiation' (for it does not reveal the final meaning of enlightenment).

(*Commentary:* The meaning of the vase initiation is that the disciple is introduced to the five Buddha families. This implies that his ordinary psychophysical aggregates of form, feeling, distinguishing awareness, volitional archetypes and the primary consciousnesses are purified and transformed into the nature of the five meditational Buddhas—Akshobya and so forth. Concurrently the five psychic poisons—ignorance, anger and so forth—are transformed into the five pristine wisdoms—mirror like wisdom, the wisdom of equanimity, etc.

The nature of the secret initiation is that the master sits in union, unites the male and female forces and gives the disciple a taste of the mystic nectars. The disciple, not understanding this secret process, is blindfolded and not permitted to watch. Therefore it is called 'the secret initiation'. Thus sharing in the master's experience, the disciple himself experiences great bliss.

In the wisdom initiation the disciple is given a knowledge lady and is instructed to sit in union. The meaning is that his mind is here introduced to its ultimate nature, or emptiness. This is symbolised by the vagina of the consort.

Generally the meaning of the fourth initiation is that the disciple's mind is introduced to the final meaning of enlightenment. Therefore it is said that only a perfect Buddha is able to actually give this initiation.)

The first three of the higher-than-higher initiations that follow are as in the previous set, with the exception that on each occasion the sexual union is performed with nine rather than one consort. As for the fourth initiation, it possesses the full characteristics of a fourth initiation and thus is called 'the non-worldly fourth initiation'.

THE PATH TO BE MEDITATED UPON

This will be presented under three headings: the vows and commitments to be maintained by a Kalachakra initiate; on the basis of this discipline, how to meditate on the generation stage yogas; and, having thus ripened one's stream of being, how to meditate upon the completion stage yogas.

THE VOWS AND COMMITMENTS TO BE MAINTAINED

These should be known from either the long or short versions
of (Tsong Kapa's) *Treatise on the Root Downfalls*.

(*Commentary:* Generally speaking, in the two Lower Tantras
one takes refuge and the common Mahayana precepts, and in
Yoga Tantra also takes the commitments of the five meditational Buddhas. In Highest Tantra one takes the fourteen
root and eight secondary precepts, as well as any precepts
unique to the tantra in question. For example, a practitioner
of the Kalachakra system has twenty-five special commitments.

It is said that if one guards one's tantric precepts and
intensely practises the yogas of generation and completion
stages, enlightenment is easily won in this very lifetime. Even
should we not accomplish these two yogas, merely guarding
the tantric precepts and practising as well as we can, guaran-
tees enlightenment within seven lifetimes. Finally, someone
who receives an initiation into Highest Tantra and guards
the commitments but does not engage in the yogas of the
two stages will nonetheless gain enlightenment within sixteen
lifetimes.)

THE GENERATION STAGE YOGAS

The degree to which one practises the generation stage
yogas is the degree to which one prepares the basis to be
purified and ripens one's mindstream for the higher yogas.
The meditator who has accomplished the generation stage
yogas will have little difficulty in mastering the yogas of the
completion stage. Thus its purpose is one of speed in the
attainment of enlightenment.

However, meditation upon solitary Kalachakra alone is
not enough to bring about the desired purification. One should
use either the complete mandala (of body, speech and mind),

or one such as the mind mandala, which incorporates symbolism revealing all stages of evolution and dissolution of the basis to be purified.

(*Commentary:* This applies to solitary Kalachakra but not solitary Vajrabhairava, or Yamantaka, whose symbolism reveals yogic methods from both male and female tantra.)

There are three Kalachakras to be meditated upon: outer, inner and alternative. Of these, outer and inner Kalachakra are the basis to be purified, whereas alternative Kalachakra refers to the yogic practices that effect this purification and produce the three purified results.

External Kalachakra means the outer world which is the vessel supporting the living beings. Thus it includes the planets of this solar system as well as the sun, moon, stars and so on. Inner Kalachakra refers to the living beings of the world, such as human beings, who are born from a womb, and who possess the six elements. Here the basis to be purified includes the aggregates, spheres of perception, channels, mystic drops and so forth of these beings. One meditates upon these two Kalachakras in order to free them from obscurations.

These are the outer and inner Kalachakras, the bases to be purified. Because they are thus associated with the path and its result, they may be subsumed under the classification of alternative Kalachakra.

In this context Kalachakra has three aspects: the methods of purifying the internal bases; those for purifying the external bases; and the methods of proceeding in the generation stage practices which ripen one's mind for the completion stage.

The wheel of protection is not applied to the basis of purification. One begins by worshipping the field of assembly and so forth, which is similar to generating the positive karma that produces rebirth with a special body in future lives. One

then recites the passage, "Because there is no inherent existence there is no inherent meditation. Meditation that grasps
at inherent existence (of meditation) is not real meditation.
Similarly; the things that we perceive are all non-existent."
Having pronounced this, one meditates on the stages of dissolution of the dual appearance of the world and its in-
habitants and then concentrates directly on the four doors
of liberation (emptiness, signlessness, wishlessness and non-
activity). This is similar to the dissolution of the physical
elements during the death of someone who has created much
positive karma and whose death is followed by the conscious
experience of clear light.

One then proceeds with the five purifications. This begins
with the visualization of the space-like *dharmadayo*. (In other
tantras this is an inverted pyramid, a three dimensional "Star of
David," or the like.) In Kalachakra, however, it is symbolised
by empty space, which is the vagina of a woman. (Just as we
humans issue forth from the vagina of our mother, the mandala
of Kalachakra issues forth from the wisdom of emptiness.)

Inside of this is the air mandala, which is related to the
area between the crown and forehead of the mother. Above
the air mandala is the mandala of fire, associated with the area
from the forehead to the throat. Above this is the water
mandala, associated with the area from the throat to the heart.
Above this is the mandala of earth, which is related to the
area between the heart and navel of the mother. Above this
is Mount Meru, associated with the area from the navel to
the anus. Above this is a lotus, associated with the area
between the anus and vagina. Above this is a moon, sun, and
fire of time, associated with the three energy channels leading
to the mother's most secret pressure point.

Above this is the vajra tent, symbolic of the father's act
of placing his vajra in the secret place of the mother. Inside
the vajra tent is the inconceivable mansion, the secret place

of the mother; and inside this the vowels and consonants of the Sanskrit alphabet stand upright upon cushions of moon and sun discs. From the moon and the sun arise the white and red bodhiminds, symbolic of the mixing of sperm and ovum in the secret place of the mother.

Between the moon and sun appears the letter *Hum*, symbolic of the entrance of a *bardo* being into the newly fertilized ovum mixture. This is marked by a black letter *Hrih*, symbolising the vital energies (produced by the fusion of sperm and ovum) which act as the vehicle of consciousness (symbolised by the letter *Hum*).

These all merge together and transform into the letter *Ham*, symbolic of the growth of the body in the womb of the mother. The letter *Ham* then transforms into light and re-emerges as Kalachakra, Lord of the Mandala, having all features.

The stages of meditation that follow, until the final generation of all the deities of the mandala, symbolise the complete evolution of the foetus, including the five aggregates, five elements, six sensory powers, six spheres of perception and five powers of action.

When the meditation approaches the time of victorious activity, the wisdom-energies arise from within one's heart and emanate with vajra wrath. This summons the Wisdom Beings of the supporting and supported Kalachakra mandalas from their natural abodes, who come and merge with the previously visualised Commitment Beings, becoming of one taste with them.

This stage of meditation until the completion of the victorious activities represents the growth of the body and the experience of sensuality. One then generates the various knowledge ladies as consorts, consecrates the vajra of the male and the lotus of the females and meditates that they enter into sexual union. This causes the letter *Ham* to melt

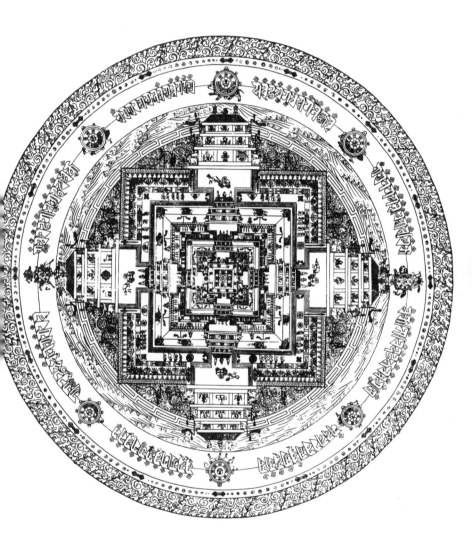

and fall from its abode at the crown and to descend (through the pressure points of the body), giving rise to the four joys. Eventually it comes to the tip of the jewel, where it is retained.

This is the yoga of the mystic drop of simultaneously arising bliss and (wisdom of) emptiness.

The mystic drop is then drawn back up to the crown, which is the yoga of subtle meditation upon bliss and emptiness.

The conventional symbol for these experiences is a sixteen year old maiden with a special sensitivity for sexual ecstasy.

THE COMPLETION STAGE YOGAS

The following explanation of the completion stage yogas will be given under three headings: the characteristics of the vajra body upon which the yogas are concentrated; a general explanation of how these six yogas are used in this application; and a detailed explanation of the yogas.

The first of these involves three subjects: the abiding channels, the flowing winds, and the bodhimind substances that are to be directed.

The discussion of the energy channels involves three subjects: the nature of the six main channels and the six main pressure points at which these converge; how these pressure points are stimulated through the six branched yoga; and an outline of which of the six yogas is applied to which of the six pressure points.

THE SIX CHANNELS AND SIX PRESSURE POINTS

The three main energy channels are called *ro-ma*, *kyang-ma*, and *dhuti*. These begin at the tip of the sexual organ, proceed back to the anus and then run straight up the centre of the body with the occasional slight bend. Eventually they come to the inside of the cranium and then curve down, terminating respectively at the top of the nostril passages and at the pillar between these.

These three are divided into upper and lower portions. The upper central channel, called *dra-chan* (the planet *Rahula*), *nyi-pang* and *abadhuti,* actually begins just above the navel. Associated with the element space, it is greenish in colour and its main function is to cause the descent of vital energy in the body. To the right of this is *ro-ma,* also called *rasana* and *nyima* (the sun). Red in colour, it is associated with the element fire and its main function is to cause blood to descend.

(*Commentary:* Here blood refers to the female substances in our body that have evolved from the original drop of ovum coming from our mother at the time of conception. Thus it exists in males as well as in females.)

To the left of this is *kyang-ma,* which is also called *la-lana* and *da-wa* (the moon). White in colour, it is associated with the element water and its main function is to cause the male fluids to descend.

(*Commentary:* Again, this includes the substances evolved from the original drop of sperm coming from one's father at the time of conception, and therefore also exists in females.)

All three of these energy channels are dominated by the life supporting energies flowing within them.

Below the navel, the central channel curves to the right and comes to the tip of the sexual organ. Here it is called *kun-dar-ma, dung-chan* and *du-me* (the planet Kalagni Rahula). Associated with wisdom, its colour is blue and its main function is to cause sperm to descend.

The left channel also curves to the centre and comes to the tip of the organ. Called *lug,* it is black in colour and is associated with the air element. Its main function is to cause urine to descend.

The right channel curves to the left and comes to the anus. Its name is *mar-ser*, and it is associated with the earth element. Yellow in colour, its main function is to cause waste products to descend.

All three of these channels are conditioned by the downward moving energies flowing within them.

Sometimes the downward moving energies may flow into the upper channels and the life supporting energies flow into the lower, giving rise to many unpleasant and dangerous conditions, such as violent disease. If such dramatic effects can be produced through (incorrect) application, then why should correct application not have similarly powerful results in the opposite direction?—results such as eliminating physical diseases and destroying the causes of death.

In the *Kalachakra Tantra*, the six pressure points, or *chakras*, are as follows. The first is located just below the crown aperture of the skull and has four petals of energy channels. The second is at the forehead and has sixteen petals. The third is located at the throat and has thirty-two petals. The fourth, which has eight petals, is at the heart. The fifth has sixty-four and is located at the navel. The sixth has two branches: the first at the anus, with thirty-two petals, and the second at the centre of the jewel, with eight petals.

At the pressure points, the left channel coils clockwise around the central channel, and the right counterclockwise, thus forming two knots that obstruct the free flow of vital energies.

One should also know how these channels converge at the pressure points and how they affect the flow of vital energies. This may be studied in larger commentaries. The nature and binding effect of these knots upon the subtle energies of the body should be studied from the "Chapter on Wisdom" of the *Abbreviated Tantra*.

In other tantras it is often said that when the side channels form knots around the central channel, they do so very tightly, leaving no space whatsoever in the coils. In Kalachakra, however, one visualises the knots as being loose and as having space between the coils.

HOW THE PRESSURE POINTS ARE STIMULATED

There are many different methods for generating tantric experience by means of drawing the male and female substances as well as the vital energies through the centre of the pressure points as explained above and for opening the central channel from top to bottom. These may be learned in detail from larger commentaries. The essence is as follows.

THE SIX YOGAS AND THE SIX PRESSURE POINTS

When practising the first two yogas—those of *sense withdrawal* and *meditative stabilization*—one concentrates the energies and drops at the upper aperture of the central channel. During the *yogas of energy concentration* and *postrecollection* one focusses these at the navel. The *yoga of retention* brings them into the central channel running through the centre of all six pressure points. Finally, by means of the *yoga of samadhi* the energies are concentrated from the base to the top of the central channel.

THE FLOWING ENERGIES

Although there is a lot of talk about the five root and five secondary energies, both of these categories share the same nature. All ten can actually be subsumed under the five root energies.

The general nature of their flow has much the same explanation in the Kalachakra system as in other Highest

Tantras (such as Yamantaka, Heruka, etc.) with the exception that Kalachakra states that fundamentally the all-pervading energy flows mainly through the gates of the nostrils.

Where are these energies generated and where do they abide? Ten energy channels converge at the heart. The two apertures of the central channel, above and below the knots at the heart, are the respective sites where the life sustaining and downward moving airs arise and abide. As for the pathways of their flow, the life sustaining energy mostly flows in the three upper channels and the downward moving through the three lower channels.

Similarly, the petals to the east and southeast of the heart are the sites of the equally abiding and *ru-pel* energies. The south and southwest are the sites of the upward moving and *tsang-pa*. The north and northeast petals are the sites of the all pervading energy and *lha-chin*. The western and north western petals are the sites of *lu* and *nor-lae-gyal*.

These flow through the major ten channels, which then subdivide into many smaller channels and eventually pervade the entire body like a fine network of interconnected passageways.

THE BODHIMIND SUBSTANCES TO BE DIRECTED

This involves three subjects: how at the time of conception the body is formed from the white and red bodhimind substances, or white and red drops; how these evolve during one's life; and how they move at the time of death.

The *Kalachakra Tantra* speaks of three types of drop-like substances: the drops generated on the four occasions (waking, dreaming, deep sleep and sexual climax); the drops of body, speech, mind and wisdom; and the drops of form, sound, thought and pristine awareness. These terms have the same referents, and their sites, nature and functions are to be realised and controlled.

The site of the drop called *the waking state, the body* and *form* is at the forehead. The site of the drop of *the dream state, speech* and *sound* is at the throat. The site of the drop of *deep sleep, mind* and *thought* is at the heart. Finally, the site of the drop of *sexual climax, wisdom* and *pristine awareness* is at the navel.

Again, the procedure of working with these drops is to bring them down from above through the central channel to the centre of the tip of the jewel, beginning with the waking state drop and eventually uniting with the drop of pristine awareness.

Moreover, when the drop of the fourth occasion melts and the collective substances are brought through the pressure points at the navel and jewel, one experiences especially great bliss. The reason for this is that the drop of the fourth occasion is associated with these two points.

The forehead and the jewel are the main sites of the white bodhimind substances, and here the red substances are weaker. The actual abode of the white substances, which act as the basis increasing the male energies, is the chakra at the forehead.

The main sites of the red bodhimind substances are the pressure points of the navel, throat and secret place, and here the white bodhimind is weaker.

At the pressure point located at the heart the two substances abide with equal strength. As explained in the *Vajra Rosary Tantra*, the mixture of white and red drops that abide in each of these pressure points are visualised as being the size of a sesame seed.

In the Kalachakra tradition all obscurations are categorised within the drops of the four occasions. What is the nature of these obscurations? The drops are focal points for the extremely subtle energies and states of consciousness, and the instincts of obscurations actually abide upon these. These instincts give rise to the obscurations to liberation (or the host of 84,000 delusions) and the obscurations to knowledge. Thus although the drops are composed of atoms (and therefore cannot actually function as a basis of obscuration, in that they act as focal points of the subtle energies and states of consciousness which carry the instincts of obscurations), to speak of them in this way is reasonable.

It is said that when one generates a drop of both the waking and fourth occasion states at the navel one experiences these two occasions (i.e. wakefulness and sexual climax) and stimulates their instincts. As for the drop at the heart, it represents the body in which one experiences deep sleep.

The way in which these four drops cause us to experience the four occasions is as follows. When the coarse energies absorb into the pressure points at the jewel and heart, one experiences deep sleep. When these energies arise and enter into both the throat and secret place, one experiences very clear dreams for a prolonged period of time. Should these energies move to the navel and forehead, one wakes from sleep and is able to perceive the manifest objects of the external world.

This shows that control of these energies and drops has a great effect on our stream of being, and that if one is able to apply the skilful yogas of the tantric path one can control one's states of consciousness. These methods of working with the subtle energies and consciousness, which have the ability to produce the qualities of Buddhahood in a single lifetime, are exclusive to Highest Yoga Tantra.

For ordinary beings the four drops carry the potency of inducing perception of the impure objects of the world, the potency of causing confused appearances and sound to arise, and the potencies giving rise to obscurity of mind, ignorance and perishable happiness. The aim of the Kalachakra yogas is to take these impure and obscured bases and to transform them into the path to enlightenment. To be specific, these three potencies are to be purified and transformed into the empty body, unconfused sound and unchanging bliss. These are cultivated to perfection, giving rise to the body, speech and mind of a Buddha and to ultimately pristine awareness.

How do the six yogas purify the bases? The stains generated on the occasion of sleep are purified and transformed into a similitude of the path by a concentrated application of the yogas of sense withdrawal, meditative stabilization and recollection. The drop of sleep is purified and transformed into the path through the yoga of energy concentration and retention. The drops of sleep and sexual climax are purified through the combined yogas of post-recollection and samadhi and are thus turned into a similitude of the path.

In the first of these purifications the yoga of sense withdrawal eliminates the stains of the drop generated in the waking state of the forehead. The yoga of post-recollection eliminates the stains of the waking drop at the navel, and, used in another way, also purifies the stains of the drop of sexual climax.

As explained above, the drop at the navel carries the potencies of generating both waking and sexual climax experiences (so this combined yogic approach is necessary).

A GENERAL EXPLANATION OF HOW THE SIX YOGAS ARE TO BE APPLIED.

Upon what tantric texts and Indian commentaries are these six yogas based? The extensive version of the *Root Tantra* (that Buddha taught to Chandrabhadra) that Chandrabhadra took to Shambhala never came back to India and consequently has never appeared in Tibet. Therefore when we Tibetans speak of the *Root Tantra* we actually are referring to the *Treatise on the Initiations*, which is only one section of the actual *Root Tantra*.

The main works by later Indian masters that are used as the basis of this tradition are Naropa's *Commentary to the Treatise on the Initiations;* (Acharya Pundarika's) *Abbreviated Tantra;* the three scriptures called *Three Commentaries on the Mind* (i.e. Chandrabhadra's *Great Commentary* and so forth); the Mahasiddha Anupamarakshita's *Six Yogas;* Suryashri's commentary to this; Shawari's *Six Yogas;* and so forth. Thus the tradition is rooted in many flawless scriptures written by unexcelled yogis of the past.

The explanation of the six yogas will discuss their groupings, their numbers, and then their stages.

The first of these subjects involves four topics: the names of the six yogas; how these six yogas become the four branches of approach and accomplishment; how they are grouped into the threefold vajra yoga and the threefold virtue; and how they are grouped into the three branches of attainment.

The names of the six yogas are: sense withdrawal, meditative stabilization, energy concentration, retention, postrecollection and samadhi, or absorption.

Generally speaking, the first two yogas are grouped together as the approach. The third and fourth yogas combine as the proximate accomplishment. The fifth yoga is the accomplishment; and the sixth is the great accomplishment, the attainment of *mahasiddhi.*

The threefold vajra yoga and the threefold virtue is explained as follows. In the beginning of practice the first two yogas become the virtuous vajra body yoga; in the middle, the third and fourth yogas become the virtuous vajra speech yoga. Finally, the fifth and sixth become the virtuous vajra mind yoga. Sometimes this last category is subdivided into two, at which time the fifth yoga is associated with the vajra mind and the sixth with the pristine vajra awareness.

The six yogas can also be divided into three groups of branches. The first two combine as the branch which accomp-

lishes form; the third and fourth as the branch which accomplishes higher energy; and the fifth and sixth yogas as the branch
which accomplishes bliss. That is, through application of the
first two yogas we produce a previously unknown form and,
by means of making this accomplishment firm, we attain an
empty body.

One then engages the yoga of energy concentration and applies a special technique in order to direct the life sustaining
and downward moving energies to the navel pressure point,
where they are brought together and used to gain control over
the other energies. After this, the yoga of retention is applied
to bring the energies of all the pressure points to the navel as
before. Thus the function of these two yogas is to establish
the branch of gaining control over the vital forces. This produces
the basis of higher energy.

When the empty body has been thus established through the
first two yogas and the basis of higher energy through the third
and forth, one applies the yoga of post-recollection to the empty
body and attains the ability to arise in the form of Kalachakra
and Consort. At that time there appear the forms of the various
empty body goddesses. This process is known as "empty body
mahamudra." The yogi, who himself has arisen in the form of
the empty body deity, then sexually unites with these goddesses,
giving rise to the extra-ordinary, supreme, unchanging bliss.
This is the fruition and final experience of the yoga of samadhi.
Therefore the fifth and six yogas are grouped together as the
branch producing bliss.

(*Commentary:* A speciality of the *Kalachakra Tantra* is
the generation of the empty body, which, as we shall see later
in the text, is somewhat equivalent to the astral body generated
in tantric systems such as Guhyasamaja, Chakrasambara and
Yamantaka. Here Gyalwa Gendun Drub says, "previously
unknown form," as the basis of the empty body has to be
produced for the first time. This is unlike the astral body,

the basis of which is the subtle energies that we have had from beginningless time.)

THE NUMBER OF THE YOGAS

As we can see from the above description, once one has accomplished the first four yogas one engages the fifth and gains the potency of the complete characteristics of an empty body. This in turn leads to the yoga of samadhi. Thus the six yogas by themselves have the power to generate the attainment of full enlightenment. There is no need to supplement them with various assortments of other practices, nor to practise anything on top of them. On the other hand, to practise less than the six yogas will not lead to final enlightenment.

THE STAGES OF THE SIX YOGAS

The six yogas are practised in the order listed above. That is, one gains stability in the first before proceeding to the second, and so forth. To practise the second before accomplishing the first will produce no results.

In the Kalachakra system the special nature of the empty body is more or less equivalent to the astral body in other tantras, with the exception that one must actually create its basis rather than merely collect the basis from a phenomenon already existing within us (i.e. such as the subtle energies used in the *Guhyasamaja Tantra*, and so forth, in order to establish an astral body). As said earlier, the first yoga produces this empty body and the second makes it firm. The third and fourth yogas are then used to gain control over the most subtle energies of the body. One then relies upon the tantric use of a consort, performs the yoga of post-recollection and arises in the empty body form of Kalachakra and Consort. This gives rise to the bliss that is the yoga of samadhi abiding in union.

Here the empty body produced by the yoga of post-recollection is similar to the astral body, or the third level of the completion stage yogas of popular tantric paths such as Guhyasamaja. The yoga of samadhi is like the yoga of Great Union in the other tantras, although it is associated with various levels of attainment. Just as (in Guhyasamaja and so forth) one first generates the Great Union of merely the superior stage, from the time one first generates the yoga of samadhi until this yoga is fulfilled one must experience the twelve levels of the 21,600 types of unchanging bliss, the first level of which is the ordinary stage. This is like the semblant astral body of the Guhyasamaja system, which is produced by the yoga of body isolation. Then, just like (in other tantras) one cultivates the yoga of mind isolation and eventually arrives at the third level (i.e., the actual astral body), in Kalachakra one applies the yoga of meditative stabilization in order to attain a semblant empty body and then cultivates this until the yoga of retention is fulfilled. Finally as an effect of the yoga of post-recollection one abandons all aspects of ordinary physical being and arises solely on the basis of the Kalachakra empty body.

A DETAILED EXPLANATION OF THE SIX YOGAS

(1) *The Yoga of Sense Withdrawal*

This will be explained under seven headings: (a) the meaning of the name of the yoga; (b) the place for performing the meditation: (c) the time for the meditation; (d) the position of the body; (e) the manner of glancing; (f) entering the suchness of mind; and (g) the signs of progress.

(a) The yoga of sense withdrawal is so called because its main function is to cut off the activity of vital energies in the six sensory organs and the six spheres of sensory perception and to bring these energies into the central channel. As is said in the fourth chapter of the *Abbreviated Tantra*, "In the yoga of sense withdrawal, the vital energies are not allowed to divert into the objects or object perceivers." The meaning is that the flow of energies to the diverse sites of sensory perception are cut off and the energies concentrated in the central channel.

How is this effected? As is said in the *Treatise on Severing the Connections*, "The method is not the simple application of attentive mindfulness (as is done in the Sutrayana path). Merely holding the mind in one-pointed concentration upon mental awareness is not enough to withdraw the subtle energies from the organs of sensory awareness. Holding the mind on a second object does not have the power to cause it to withdraw from other objects." The reason is that a mere mental application is not strong enough to eliminate the activity of the subtle energies in the sensory spheres. Therefore in the Kalachakra yogas one stimulates the points of the body through which the vital energies flow, causing them to be diverted from the sensory powers and to enter into the central channel, where they abide and then dissolve. Through this effort the sensory awareness based upon these energies is reversed and their connection to the mental awareness severed.

(b) The place for practising this meditation is an extremely dark room.

(c) The yoga is actually to be applied when the earth energy courses most strongly in the right nostril. This is said to be the time when the energies of the sensory spheres are most easily withdrawn.

(d) The position in which one should sit to perform the yoga of sense withdrawal is either the *vajra* or *sattva* positions. The hands are formed into vajra fists with the finger knuckles facing upwards and the back of the hands pressed tightly against the two major arteries of the thighs. The elbows are kept tightly against the body and the back totally straight.

One should sit in this position without moving for the entire session, regardless of what pains come into the limbs, eyes and so forth.

(e) Progress in the yoga of sense withdrawal is accompanied by the ten signs. These arise inside *abadhuti*, the central channel. As is said in the fifth chapter of the *Abbreviated Tantra*, "....until one sees a flicker of stainless black light inside the channel."

Chandrabhadra's *Great Commentary* states, "....until the signs appear in *abadhuti*, the channel of time."

Also, the "Chapter on Wisdom" (in the) A*bbreviated Tantra* says, "The signs do not appear externally, such as in the sky. The eyes are partially closed, a glance cast upward and the signs observed in the central channel."

The *Great Commentary* states, "One glances at the vajra path. When the vital energies enter into the centre of this and only emptiness is experienced, one sees the signs such as smoke." The meaning is that by bringing the vital energies into the central channel, holding them there and then dissolving them, one gradually attains the ten signs of progress, such as smoke, etc.

As said above, the eyes and the mind should focus upon the central channel at the point where it passes through the pressure point of the forehead. The "Chapter on Accomplishment" (i.e. Chapter IV of the *Abbreviated Tantra*) says, "The yogi performing the propitiation casts a wrathful glance at the pressure point associated with the space element. This glance, called 'the destroyer of demons,' is focused on the path of nectar, (i.e. the pressure point of the forehead, where the nectar-like sperm coming from one's father is retained). One then looks for the signs of proximate attainment."

Chandrabhadra's commentary adds, "By the wrathful glance at the crown, the eyes partially closed and looking upwards, the signs appear." Thus the wrathful glance of the eyes during the yoga of sense withdrawal and meditative stabilization is called "the glance that destroys demons."

The action of destroying demons refers to the swirling of the sperm-like nectar. This is the bodhimind substance which is found in the pressure point located at the forehead. The reason for casting the glance at this spot is that by the yogas of sense withdrawal and meditative stabilization one produces the basis of the empty body for the first time and then makes this attainment firm. As said earlier, the drop of the waking state is located at the pressure point of the crown. By concentrating and meditating on this, all of the various objects that manifest to the mind on the basis of this drop, together with the perceptual instincts, are severed. When this occurs, the empty body is easily produced.

As for the signs themselves, the *Guhyasamaja Tantra* states, "The first is like smoke, the second like a mirage, the third like **radiant fireflies**, the fourth like a blazing butter-lamp and the fifth like the space of clouds."

Also the *Arali Tantra* states, "The eyes are held half closed and a glance cast upward at the point between the eyebrows." The meaning is that the yogi casts a glance up to the centre of the eyebrows and focusses his mind one-pointedly on the empty space of the upper aperture of the central channel, thus concentrating the vital energies. Here, space refers to that inside the crown pressure point. Awareness should not be allowed to wander elsewhere.

(f) Through the yogas of energy concentration and retention, the vital energies are brought under control and directed into the central channel. This causes the fires of the mystic heat to blaze upward and to melt the substances, giving rise to great bliss. This consciousness of great bliss is then directed into meditation upon suchness.

The purpose here is not to establish a meditation upon suchness as a cause sharing the nature of the *Dharmakaya*, but to fulfil the yogas of sense withdrawal and meditative stabilization with which one previously accomplished and then made firm a semblance of the empty body.

(g) Many levels of signs appear during the yoga of sense withdrawal and meditative stabilization, beginning with those that arise when one concentrates the energies at the doors of the organs and so forth. At this point in practice, the signs seem to arise in one's meditation hut.

Next one brings the energies into the central channel for the first time. The signs of this experience appear at various places throughout the body, but not inside the central channel itself. Only when one has produced the basis of the empty body will they appear in the space of the upper aperture of the central channel as explained above.

The scriptures state that four signs arise during the day and six during the night, elucidating the manner of their appearance with certainty. The signs appear consecutively, and the third must arise before the fourth, etc. Each stage of practice must be made clear and firm before proceeding to the next.

The *Guhyasamaja Tantra* states that the signs first arise at the eyebrows. The *Kalachakra Tantra* adds that because there are various types and levels of energies, there are also various places and times for the manifestation of the signs. For example, when the yogi cuts off the flow of the vital energies passing through the four petals of the four intermediate directions at the heart *chakra*, or the *ru-pel*, *tsang-pa*, *lha-chin*, and *nor-lay-gyal* energies, he experiences the signs of smoke, a mirage, radiant fireflies and a butter lamp. When he halts the flow of the equally abiding, upward flowing, all pervading and *lu* energies that flow through the four petals of the cardinal directions, he perceives the signs of Kalagni, the moon, the sun and Rahula.

One then cuts off the flow of the life sustaining and downward moving energies which course above and below, thus experiencing the signs of lightning and the primordial drop.

To prepare oneself for the completion stage practices

through which one experiences these signs of controlling the ten energies in the production of the empty body, one first practices the generation stage method of visualising the ten powerful goddesses at the *chakra* of bliss. Similarly, in the generation stage yogas the Lord Kalachakra and Consort are visualised as representing the element space and wisdom, respectively. Their sexual union coincides with the completion stage meditations upon the union of the two main energies flowing within these.

This generation of the ten vital energies of the student as the powerful goddesses is associated with the initiation of the silk headress.

After the ten signs have been experienced, a small black line the size of a hair appears in the mystic drop. This signifies the attainment of the five certainties of the *Sambhogakaya*. However, these five certainties do not have the same meaning as in the other scriptures. What are they in the Kalachakra system? The certain time is at the end of the complete ten signs, and the certain place is inside the central channel. The certain nature is that this body is not based upon either coarse or subtle atoms but is produced purely by mental images. The certain body is that of Vajrasattva. Finally, the certain aspect is the blissful eternal kiss of the male and consort.

The complete manifestation of all ten signs and the attainment of the above body having the five certainties, marks the completion of the powers of the yoga of sense withdrawal. It also marks the point at which one should take up the second of the six yogas, i.e. that of meditative stabilization.

The reason for practising the yoga of sense withdrawal in both daily and nightly yogas is that various of the signs are more easily attained at different moments. For example, the empty body is easily attained in darkness and is very difficult to generate in brightness. Moreover, when one casts the glance and holds the visualizations (as explained previously), it

is difficult to cut off the flow of energies in the eye power
when the atmosphere is bright.   These energies are spontaneously stimulated by the effect of colour and so forth.
This agitating influence is not present in times of darkness.

THE YOGA OF MEDITATIVE STABILIZATION

The physical position for performing the yoga of meditative
stabilization is as previously explained.

Through application of this yoga one fills the skies with the
various empty bodies and symbols previously generated within
the mystic drop.

One then dissolves all these gods into one another and then
into the Beatific Form of the *Sambhogakaya* as explained
above, establishing the special divine pride until it effortlessly arises. When this divine pride dominates one's entire
being, the yoga of meditative stabilization has been attained.
One then is ready to enter into the third of the six yogas, that
of energy concentration.

The yoga of meditative stabilization has five branches.
Respectively, these are called conceptualization, experience,
joy, bliss, and one-pointedness.

The meaning of these is given by Naropa in his *Commentary
to the Treatise on the Initiations*, "Seeing merely the nature
of the coarse empty body is conceptualization; seeing deeply
into the nature of the subtle empty body is experience. The
feelings associated with the mental consciousnesses which arise
from the pliancy of mind thus effected give rise to joy. The
feelings associated with the physical consciousness arising
from the pliancy of body give rise to bliss. Finally, the images
of mind that arise in the form of Vajrasattva possessing the
five certainties are inseparably mixed with the inner nature
of one's own mind, giving rise to a consciousness which is an
inseparable unity of form and thought. This is the branch of

one-pointedness." The first two of these five branches combine as the practice of *vipassyana,* or insight meditation, and the last three as *samatha,* or meditative serenity. The fulfillment of the five produces the samadhi which is the inseparable unity of insight and serenity.

THE YOGA OF ENERGY CONCENTRATION

The meaning of the words *energy concentration* is that one arrests the flow of energies passing through the right and left channels and concentrates them in the central channel. The reason for doing this yoga is that although one previously generated the pride of establishing the empty body within the central channel and uniting it inseparably with the deeper nature of one's mind, there still remains a distance between these and certain of the vital energies. Therefore one must sever this and generate a firm and unfeigned pride of Vajrasattva's form, applying the energy yogas to the pressure points of the body as explained earlier.

In the yoga of energy concentration one brings these to the pressure point at the navel and causes the mystic heat to blaze forth with special strength. It flares up the central channel, melts the substances of bodhimind and gives rise to an experience of unprecedented great bliss. One must here apply special techniques in order to bring the life sustaining and downward moving energies to the navel and to unify them accordingly.

The two main techniques used to bring about this union is the vajra recitation and the vase breathing. The method for applying these two yogic techniques for concentrating, holding and dissolving the vital energies are explained in the *Commentary to the Praise of Vajrapani.* One begins by performing the vajra recitation until one's mind becomes clear and the elements relaxed. This causes the vital energies to flow especially smoothly. One then changes to meditation upon vase breathing.

There are many Tibetan traditions for applying the vajra recitation. Some yogis have said that when the air passes through both nostrils it should be visualised as entering into the two side and also the central channel. It should then be visualised as entering, abiding and dissolving within the three channels in the form of the three letters *Om, Ah* and *Hum* while the three channels are visualised as the vajra body, speech and mind recitations. However this simple technique can hardly be the great vajra yoga of the Kalachakra system, which is a Highest Yoga Tantra.

In our tradition the vajra recitation is as explained in the *Commentary to the Praise of Chakrasambhara* and also Naropa's *Commentary to the Treatise on the Initiations.* When one meditates upon the yoga of energy concentration and casts the glance eliminating demons, one watches for the semblant and actual signs as explained previously in the yoga of sense withdrawal. One observes the empty body unified with the vital energies. The energies enter inside and are then made to arise with the luminosity of *Om.* This is brought to the centre of the pressure point at the crown, where rests the empty body that was previously produced through the first two yogas. This energy is then retained and made to arise with the luminosity of the letter *Hum.* Together with the empty body it is then brought to the navel. As the energies are released, they are made to arise with the luminosity of the letter *Ah.* The strength of the flowing energies causes the empty body and so forth to move up the path of the central channel to the upper aperture, where they exit.

Through repeated meditation, the inhalation and exhalation periods gradually decrease and the period of retention increases until one is eventually able to retain the application of the empty body and the vital energies at the navel for long periods of time.

After the vajra recitation technique has been mastered one can take up the practice of vase breathing. The method is as follows. The life-sustaining and downward moving energies are brought via the central channel to the navel chakra, where, together with the mind, they unite with the drop of sexual climax. These two energies, together with one's own mind and the special empty body, are brought into one-tasteness and this state of consciousness carefully maintained. One then meditates on vase breathing.

As Naropa said, "The energies above and below are brought together and kissed with the mind." One brings these energies to the navel, forms a vase and ignites the fires of the mystic heat. This gives rise to the four great blisses resulting from the falling of the mystic drop through the four principal pressure points. These in turn fulfil the powers of energy concentration yoga.

When this experience has been gained one is ready to approch the yoga of retention.

THE YOGA OF RETENTION

The technique is similar to the vase breathing meditation, although the place and stages of the meditation differ. One begins the meditation of dissolving the elements by absorbing earth into water, bringing these energies into the central channel and to the heart. Water is then dissolved into fire and brought to the throat. Next, fire is dissolved into air and brought to the forehead. Finally, air is dissolved into space and brought to the crown; and space is dissolved into wisdom and brought to the secret place. One then performs the meditation on the inseparability of the life-sustaining and downward moving energies, the mind and the empty body. Meditating in this way one transfers the vase-like collection of energies and retains them at each of the pressure points as described above. This gives rise to the four joys caused by moving the mystic drop and so forth through the pressure points from below upward. One then uses these joys as the basis of the meditation upon the union of bliss and wisdom.

As a preliminary to this exercise one must create the strong thought, "I myself have the form of Kalachakra and Consort." The power of this thought gives one the ability to perform the above yogas on the basis of the semblant empty body.

The presentation of the Kalachakra yoga of retention is similar to that of the clear light yoga as found in other tantric systems such as Guhyasamaja. Its special function is to purify the drop of sexual climax from obscurations. By creating an inseparable union of the two main energies, one's mind and also the empty body, and then concentrating these at each of the six pressure points, one carries the yoga of retention to completion and arrives at the threshold of the yoga of post-recollection.

THE YOGA OF POST-RECOLLECTION

The yoga of post-recollection, also known as the vajra mind yoga, is a method for producing the special Kalachakra bliss. The etymology of its name is given in the *Great Commentary*, "One recollects a reflection of the form previously accomplished and then applies special mindfulness to it." The meaning here is that through the previous yogas one arose as the lustful empty body gods and goddesses of the mandala and experienced divine pride, and the deities filled the realms of the world with lights and entered into union; yet this did not give rise to the unchanging bliss. Therefore the attainment was called 'the semblant astral body.' One persists in the meditation until the mind spontaneously arises in the empty body form of Kalachakra and Consort. This causes lights to emanate from one's pores, arousing the desire of the empty body *mahamudra*, such as the Five Consorts and Ten Powerful Goddesses. One then enters into union with these goddesses and experiences the unchanging great bliss. When one has gained the ability to dwell in a sustained awareness of this unchanging bliss, the yoga of post-recollection has been accomplished.

As for this practice, the *Great Commentary* lists four types of *mudras: karmamudra, jnanamudra, mahamudra* and *samayamudra*. The first three of these give rise to the unchanging bliss; the fourth is said to be the *mudra* experienced as a result of accomplishing the former three.

Karmamudra is explained as a maiden possessing the physical attributes of a woman, who comes to one as a result of one's previous karma. Here there is no need to visualise the experience; the maiden herself has the ability to induce the full experience by means of her skillful embrace.

Jnanamudra is a maiden created through the power of one's visualization.

As for *mahamudra*, the images within one's own mind spontaneously arise as the various consorts having an empty body. One then unites with these.

Through relying upon these three types of *mudra* one is led to the experience of bliss. The bodhimind substances abiding in the upper sites fall to the tip of the jewel, where they vibrate and transform. They are retained here and are not allowed to slip away.

The *Great Commentary* states, "*Karmamudra* is the maiden who gives one the falling bliss. *Jnanamudra* is the maiden who gives one the moving bliss. *Mahamudra* is the maiden who gives the unchanging bliss." How is this so? If the yogi is not able to move the male and female drops of his body solely through the power of meditation, he is instructed to take up the practice of *karmamudra*. Because the *karmamudra* gives him the power to direct the vital substances to the tip of the jewel, she is called "the maiden who bestows the falling bliss."

Jnanamudra: Union with her causes the drops to fall from the upper pressure points to the tip of the jewel; but as they cannot be retained motionlessly, they are directed through various other points of the body. Thus she is called "the maiden who brings the moving bliss."

Mahamudra: One sits in union with her, which causes the substances to melt and come to the tip of the jewel. Not only are these to be prevented from slipping; they must also be prevented from falling into other sites. Thus it is said, "the maiden who brings unchanging bliss."

The yogis who accomplish the actual empty body of Kalachakra and Consort are of three types: sharp, middling and dull. The first of these relies exclusively upon *mahamudra*. They are able to experience the unchanging bliss solely through union with her. The second must first rely upon *jnanamudra* to generate a basis of bliss through which they are able to enter into *mahamudra*. Thirdly, those of dull capacity, not having the strength or purity of mind, must rely upon *karmamudra* until they gain the experience of great bliss; only then can they proceed to the *mahamudra*.

In this way, all three types of yogis eventually come to the *mahamudra*. The white drop of mystic substances that abides in the crown is caused to melt and fall to the tip of the jewel. Simultaneously, the red drop moves to the pressure point at the crown. The two substances are then retained and made firm until the supremely great unchanging bliss is experienced.

It is said that this bliss arises in momentary flashes, and that it is the principal force transporting one from the yoga of post-recollection to the yoga of samadhi. A single moment of this transcendental ecstasy causes utter transformation within the atomic structure of one portion of the 21,600 facets of the physical body. Simultaneously, 1,800 of the 21,600 karmic energies coursing through the nostrils are arrested. When 1,800 experiences of bliss have been realised and 1,909 of the vital drops collected, one attains to the Supreme Dharma stage of the path of preparation, second of the five paths to enlightenment. A further 1,800 such moments places one on the stage of a High One, the path of direct vision.

If in this way one can draw 21,600 male drops to the female site and 21,600 of the female drops to the male site, one experiences 21,600 moments of bliss and cuts off 21,600 karmic winds, thus causing an equivalent degree of the atomic structure of one's body to disappear. One's form aggregate, together with the elements and objects connected with it, become freed from obscuration, and the veils to knowledge are simultaneously overcome. Thus in a single lifetime one gains the state of Buddha in the aspect of primordial Kalachakra.

The *Abbreviated Tantra* states, "When one realises the body, speech and mind produced by the path of the Kalachakra yogas, one's body transcends ordinary substantiality, becomes as clear and lucent as the sky, and manifests all the major and minor signs of perfection. One's mind fills with great bliss and one enters into an eternal embrace with the innately unmoving wisdom." The meaning here is that the Kalachakra yogi accomplishes enlightenment in one lifetime in such a way that his body attains the characteristics of the form of Kalachakra and Consort: a vast empty body adorned with all signs of enlightenment, a body similar to space itself. It is "clear and lucent" because it is intangible and immaterial, being empty of a mundane atomic structure. This is the bodily attainment. As for the mental attainment, it represents the supreme, unchanging great bliss locked in eternal union with the one-tasteness of wisdom perceiving the emptiness of non-inherent existence, which is beyond characteristics. When in this way the body and mind are experienced as an inseparable entity based on the supporting empty body and the supported wisdom of great bliss, one attains the primordial state of Kalachakra. This is the accomplishment of the yoga of samadhi, last of the six-branched Kalachakra yoga system.

In the Kalachakra literature one sees a lot of discussion concerning the terms "emptiness with characteristics" and "true emptiness without characteristics." The first of these is in reference to the mind perceiving the empty body within a subtle light of dual appearance. It is nonetheless called "emptiness" because it is based upon a mind arising from a body in which all physical characteristics have been eliminated. The second emptiness refers to the mind perceiving the emptiness of inherent existence without even a slight appearance of duality.

This method of bringing the wisdom of emptiness into one-tasteness with the supreme, unchanging great bliss is similar to the clear light teachings of other tantras. In the same context, the empty body that is accomplished is somewhat similar to the concept to the illusory body yoga in other systems. The assembling of these two elements within the body and mind (i.e., blissful wisdom and the empty body) is like the Great Union spoken of in other tantras. In Kalachakra, however, the yogi cultivates the twelve phases of 21,600 experiences of bliss and emptiness, each of which arrests 21,600 energies and dissolves 21,600 physical bases. This in turn destroys 21,600 delusions and causes 21,600 of the essential drops to collect together. Simultaneously, one is transported through the meditational experiences of the twelve stages of the higher Kalachakra paths.

In brief, if one is able to dwell in the vajra pride of the Kalachakra empty body in union with the secret place of the Consort, all energies are brought into perfect harmony in the points of the central channel from the navel to the crown.

With the exception of the theory of the empty body, and

the discussion of the boundaries of the first stages of attainment, the Kalachakra presentation of the six yogas very much resembles the *Lam Dre* doctrine (of the Sakya Sect).

Oh hark !!! This brief treatise on the six yogas
Of primordial Kalachakra's completion stage
Draws from the ancient Indian scriptures
And presents their thought without error.

Requested by several of my disciples,
I, Gendun Drub, wrote it to refresh my memory
And to express my respect for the practice
And teachings of the great yogis of old.
May it benefit those who share my fate.

May any small merits that it has
Cause the living beings to enter the secret Vajrayana
That they may be filled with the glory
Of supreme bliss and the wisdom of emptiness,
And attain to the primordial state of Buddhahood.

The Colophon : Written by Gendun Drub, an insignificant apprentice to the omniscient master Pakpa Yonten Gyatso.

BIBLIOGRAPHY OF TEXTS QUOTED

Guhyasamaja Tantra
(Tantra of the Secret Assembly)
bSang-'dus-rtsa-rgyud (T).

Vajra Rosary of Initiations
dKyil-chog-rdor-phreng (T.)

Treatise on the Initations
dBang-mdor-bstan-pa (K.)

Commentary to the Treatise on the
   Initiations
dBang-mdor-bstan-pai- 'grel-pa (T.)

Heruka Chakasambhara Tantra
bDe-mchog-rtsa-rgyud (T.)

Great Commentary
'Grel-chen (T.)

Vajra Rosary Tantra
rGyud-rdo-rje-phréng-ba (T.)

Abbreviated Tantra
bsDus-rgyud (T.)

Treatise on Cutting Off the Connections
'Brel-pa-gcod-pa (T.)

Arali Tanta
A-ra-lii-rgyud (K.)

Commentary to the Vajra Essence
rDo-rje-snying-'grel (T.)

Chapter VI:

Three Prayers

Text One: A Song to the Spiritual Master

Namo Guru Byah!

Physical presence that arouses spiritual curiosity,
A voice that causes the hair on one's body to quiver,
A mind of compassion giving rise to all excellence:
Homage to the qualified spiritual master.

A sky-like yogi watches the world around him,
His mind unmoving from space-like dharmadhatu wisdom;
Yet he acts as a peerless father to fortunate trainees:
Homage to the qualified spiritual master.

Fully experienced in the three baskets of sutra and four
    classes of tantra,
Adorned with zeal for the three higher trainings,
An embodiment of the Buddha, Dharma and Sangha:
Homage to the qualified spiritual master.

Bestowing teachings, initiations and oral transmissions,
He cuts confusion at the crossroads of unknowing.
Homage to the qualified spiritual master,
A jewel heralding liberation from samsara.

Master whose mind is free in the skies of clear light
And whose body is adorned by perfect signs of Great Union;
Bodhisattva performing the work of Buddha Vajradhara,
I send forth this request to you.

From now until all beings gain enlightenment,
Continue to manifest unceasingly in the world;
To inspire the people to learn Dharma's way
And to practise correctly, that illumination be produced.

Inspire trainees to make great efforts in meditation
And thus find the state of great bliss today.
Emanate dakinis from your body, speech and mind
To lead those who single-pointedly strive at Dharma.

The Colophon: Written one morning by Gyalwa Gendun Drub while journing to Lhagyal Tser-cho.

Text Two: A Prayer to Maitreya Buddha

May the beings who contribute to the creation
Of images of Maitreya, the Buddha of Love,
Experience the Dharma of the Great Way
In the presence of Maitreya himself.

When like a sun rising from behind the mountains,
The Buddha of Love appears at the Diamond Seat,
May the lotus of wisdom be opened
And the living beings swarm to drink truth's honey.

At that time may the Buddha of Love
Reach down with his compassionate hand
And prophesy the enlightenment of trainees,
That they may quickly gain illumination.

Until final enlightenment may living beings dwell
In the vast and profound ways followed
By the Buddhas and their sons the Bodhisattvas
Of time past, present and future.

May all beings hold wisdom's golden handle
And fly the flag of spiritual learning that is
Adorned by discipline, meditation and insight,
That the banner of truth may everywhere be seen.

May the mystic lore, a source of happiness
And all deeper evolution, thrive without hindrance;
May the holders of knowledge live for long
And may Buddha's teachings bring peace and joy to the world.

Through becoming familiar with the Buddha of Love
May the living beings gain love's splendour,
That dispels the shadows of evil;
And may they progress toward illumination.

Text Three: A Prayer to Mahakala

Nama Mahakalaya!

Homage to Mahakala, the Great Black One,
Wrathful emanation of the Bodhisattva of Compassion,

Homage to Mahakala, whose implements are
The skull-cup of blissful wisdom and the knife
Of penetrating methods severing negativity,
The Black Lord of ferocious appearance
Whose voice causes all on the earth to tremble.

O Mahakala, you appear in the form of a terrible demon
In order to overcome the endless hosts of demons.
Like the first day of the new moon,
You herald the destruction of the forces of darkness.

In the presence of the Tathagata himself you pledged
To work aganst the evil forces causing sorrow.
Homage to the fountain of protective energies
That dispel all forms of suffering
And counteract the elements obstructing life.

O Mahakala and the seventy lords in your retinue,
Yours is the power to overcome all maras
And to carry on high the victory banner of Dharma.
Yours is the power to bring joy to the world.

Protective lord whose fangs are love, compassion, equanimity
  and joy,
Whose body blazes with fires of wisdom,
Your mantra is like the roar of a lion
Causing the jackels of evil to scatter.

Homage to the protective lord who when invoked
Comes through the power of magical emanation
And out of compassion releases magical energies
That explode like the bark of a dragon.

Just as the angry yak catches its enemy on its horns
And then shakes the very life out of him,
Similarly do you destroy the inner forces
By which we obstruct our own path to liberation.

O Mahalaka, lord of the Cemetery of Laughter,
Your roar *ah-la-la, hum-hum* and *phat-phat*
Drains the malace of the enemies of goodness
And steals the very life of the devil and his agents.

Homage also to your four principal consorts:
Yung-mo, Tam-mo, Srin-mo and Sing-gali,

Wisdom emanations whose bodies are naked,
Who hold the knife of method in their right hand
And with their left hold up a skull-cup
Filled with the blood of transcendental knowledge.

O Mahakala and those in your mystic circle,
Hear this prayer of mine.
Follow close behind me like a shadow,
Protecting me in all Dharmic activities.

From now until all beings gain enlightenment,
Befriend all who practise the methods of the path.
Let no hindrances or obstructions arise
To the study or practise of spiritual ways.

Help practitioners always to have
Every condition conducive to the path,
Such as long life, health and the necessities of life,
That they may quickly attain the state of a Buddha.

  *The Colophon : Written by Gendun Drub on the occasion of
Buddha's Day of Miracles. At the time Gendun Drub was
living in retreat above Jang Chen Monastery.*

Chapter VII:

A Rosary of Spiritual Advice

O friends with intelligence and interest
   in the teachings,
Listen well to some parting advice.

Although we wander endlessly in samsara,
There is little space for lasting happiness
Because of the negativity we carry within.
Seek now for the ambrosia of immortality,
The wisdom of conventional and ultimate truth.

Keeping the body humble and at peace
And not speaking unpleasantly nor deceptively,
Absorb the mind in the spiritually beneficial.
Course in the dharmadhatu wisdom
Like a fish swimming in the ocean
Free of the hooks of desire and attachment.

The great king of trees now stands tall,
Yet certainly it will one day age and dry.
The Lord of Death shall certainly take us too,
And if we are not prepared with knowledge
We shall no doubt know terror and regret.

Like me, the countless living beings
Have been wandering in cyclic existence.
Many times they have been a parent to me
And shone radiant kindness upon me.
How unworthy not to respond to their sorrow!
For the sake of all living beings we must
Strive in the practices bringing enlightenment.

If one does not retreat to the mountains
And accomplish the profound and difficult yogas,
To refer to oneself as a yogi resembles
A jackel imitating the roar of a lion.

Forget the endless materialistic pursuits
And learn to accept whatever comes.
A precious human rebirth is gained this once;
Do not let it slip through your fingers.
I urge you, use it meaningfully.
Apply it to the spiritual path.

Do not project deceptive ways, like a
Newly cast brass statue seems to be gold.
Dwell in the vibrantly warm thought that encourages
Spiritual growth in oneself and others.

This present age rages with five degenerate conditions
Able to disrupt most paths to liberation.
The oral tradition coming from the master Atisha

Easily transforms these into causes
Generating progress within fortunate trainees.
Make contact with a qualified lineage holder
And apply yourself to the methods
That use the conditions of a world steeped in negativity
As causes of the altruistic state of knowledge.

The Colophon: Written by Gendun Drub while living in retreat above Sang-pu Monastery.

Bibliography of Texts Herein Translated

(4) A Rosary of Gems, Chapter XXIV
     Rin-chen-'phreng-ba-las-leu-nyer-bzhi-pa

Chapter IV

(5) Song of the Eastern Snow Mountains
     Shar-gang-ri-ma

Chapter V

(12) Notes on Kalachakra
     Dus-'khor-bskyed-rdzogs-zin-bris

Chapter VI

Three Prayers
(13) A Song to the Spiritual Master
     bla-mai-gsol-'debs

(14) A Prayer to Maitreya Buddha
     Byams-pa-sku-gjugs-ma

(15) A Prayer to Mahakala
     Zhal-bzhi-ka-bstod

Chapter VII

(16) A Rosary of Spiritual Advice
     Zhal-gdams-ka-'phreng

Acknowledgements

Crushing the Forces of Evil to Dust was originally translated with Chomdze Tashi Wangyal and Losang N. Tsonawa in 1977, and was published together with the Tibetan text in *The Tibet Society Bulletin*, Vol. 14, Dec. 1979, Indiana, U.S.A. The translator would like to thank the editor for permission to reprint it here. Thanks also to Mr. Graham Coleman, a poet whose editing work on this piece is most appreciated. Ven. Chomdze Tashi Wangyal also provided the commentaries to text two of Chapt. III, as well as to text three of Chapt. VI, and to the poem in Chapter VII.

Notes on Spiritual Transformation was translated with Ven. Amchok Tulku of Ganden Shartse Monastery, just before Rinpoche left for Vienna University in 1980. Rinpoche's lucid commentary to this work rendered the classical Kadampa writing style (11th-14th cen.), often quite difficult to follow due to its antiquated nature, into clear and lively prose.

Text one in Chapter II—*Turning Toward Emptiness*—was translated with Ven. Doboom Tulku, Secretary to H.H. the Dalai Lama.

My translation of *Song of the Eastern Snow Mountains* is based upon Johan Van Manen's Tibetan text, translation and commentary as published in the *Journal of the Astatic Society of Bengal*, Calcutta, 1919. This song is known by heart to most Tibetan lamas. This translator first heard it sung by Ven. Geshey Ngawang Dargye, a lord of meditators and one of Sera Monastery's foremost scholars. Gendun Drub composed both the words and melody of this piece while in a state of trance, and the tune is nothing short of transporting. Ven. Geshey Ngawang Dargye has a magnificient chanting voice, and his inspiring presentation of the number was the factor causing it to be included in this present volume.

Notes on Kalachakra was prepared with Ven. Thepo Tulku of Ganden Shartse Monastery, a young lama well versed in the scriptures and thoroughly spontaneous in his conduct. Rinpoche's teacher Lati Rinpoche kindly provided the commentary.

A Prayer to Maitreya Buddha was prepared with Gelong Hans Van der Bogert, a Dutch monk and friend.

Many thanks to Mr. Gyatso Tsering, Director of the Library of Tibetan Works and Archives, Dharamsala, for his permission to use the Library's facilities; and to the Bonpo teacher Patsen Lama Sonam Gyaltsen for loaning me several texts from his private collection that were not available anywhere in Dharamsala. Acknowledgements are also extended to Jeremy Russell, Katie Cole and Sean Jones, whose financial assistance made this production possible; and to David Stuart, who painstakingly checked the final drafts of all ten translations against the original Tibetan.

Finally, special thanks to the venerable Gelong Dr. Nick Ribush and the staff at the Tushita Mahayana Meditation Centre, New Delhi, for their hospitality and editing assistance during the final production of the work.

Illustrations: Kevin Rigby: pages 1, 2, 14, 16, 17, 33, 35, 36, 37, 39, 40, 53, 54, 60, 61, 65, 71, 75, 80, 82, 93, 94, 95, 100, 101, 109, 110, 155, 156, 157, 158, 160, 162, 164, 165, 166, 168, 173, 174; Garrey Folkes: 159; Katie Cole: 4, 41, 161; Ani Yarna: 115, 120; from Tibetan woodblocks: 18, 30 50, 120. Concerning Kevin's works, illustrations page 35, 54, 93, 110, 156, 160 and 174 are from the private collection of Michael Hellbach and are here reprinted from the German journal *Aus Tushita*.

~~~~~~

The Tashi Lhungpo Cultural Society
(Gesak Project)
P.O. Box Bylakuppe,
Mysore Dist., Karnataka, India

Tashi Lhungpo Monastery, established by the First Dalai Lama and the active seat of the Panchen Lama since the time of the Fifth Dalai Lama, was one of Tibet's four most renowned Gelukpa monastic colleges. Unlike the other great Gelugpa monasteries (Ganden, Sera and Drepung), which specialised in "the five great themes of Buddha (*Prajna-paramita, Madhyamaka, Pramana, Abhidharma* and *Vinaya*), Tashi Lhungpo took "the five great sciences" as the basis of its training programme. Included in these are astrolgy and poetry. Thus Tashi Lhungpo has served a unique function in the preservation of Tibetan culture.

Like all Tibetan monasteries, Tashi Lhungpo was forcibly closed by the Chinese communists and its monks imprisoned, killed or disrobed. Only a handful of the almost 7,000 monks that it housed have managed to escape. A small replica of the institution has been built in South India, where a half dozen masters are attempting to pass their lineages to several dozen young trainees. But as refugees in a Third World country, their task is not easy. Should they succeed, the tradition will not have been destroyed.

Anyone interested in helping this monastery by sponsoring a young monk (only $150. per year) or making a general contribution may write directly to the above address. Donations of medicines and vitamins would also be appreciated, as the change in diet and climate between the Himalayas and tropical South India has placed serious health problems upon both the aged teachers and their young students.

~~~~~~

Tibetan Scriptures Published In India

The Collected Works of Lama Tsong Khapa

Lama Tsong Khapa (1357-1419), who founded the Gelukpa Order as a synthesis of all older sects, was a prolific writer, and the eighteen volumes of his *Collected Works* cover all aspects of the Sutrayana and Vajrayana paths. These have recently been republished by Ngawang Gelek Demo in New Delhi, and the complete set is available in the Student's Edition at a cost of U.S. $200, including shipping. The superior Library Edition costs $60., per volume.

The same publisher has also brought out the *Collected Works* of Khedrub Je and Gyaltsep Je, Tsong Khapa's two chief disciples. As mentioned in *Song of the Eastern Snow Mountains*, these three teachers were most important to the spiritual life of the First Dalai Lama. Both of these collections are available at a cost of U.S. $200., shipping included.

Inquiries may be addressed to: Ngawang Gelek Demo, Defence Colony, C-Block 115, New Delhi 110024.

The Collected Works of the First Dalai Lama

Although the First Dalai Lama spent most of his life in meditation, six volumes of written works nonetheless issued forth from his pen. These have recently been published in India (*Tales of Vinaya* excepted) and are available at a cost of U.S. $350., including shipping. Inquiries may be addressed to:

Dodrub Sangye, Deorli Chorten, Gangtok, Sikkim, India.